Bees
A Natural History

Bees
A Natural History

Christopher O'Toole

Honorary Research Associate
Hope Entomological Collections
Oxford University Museum of Natural History

Featuring photographs by Edward Ross

A Peter N. Névraumont Book

FIREFLY BOOKS

A FIREFLY BOOK

Published by Firefly Books Ltd. 2013

First printing

Publisher Cataloging-in-Publication Data (U.S.)
A CIP record for this title is available from Library of Congress

Library and Archives Canada Cataloguing in Publication
A CIP record for this title is available from Library and Archives Canada

Published in the United States by
Firefly Books (U.S.) Inc.
P.O. Box 1338, Ellicott Station
Buffalo, New York 14205

Published in Canada by
Firefly Books Ltd.
50 Staples Avenue, Unit 1
Richmond Hill, Ontario L4B 0A7

Printed in Canada

Front cover image: ehabeljean © Shutterstock.com
Back cover image: StudioSmart © Shutterstock.com

Produced by Névraumont Publishing Company,
Brooklyn, New York
Design by Nicholas LiVolsi

Having established her nest, this female mason bee (*Osmia leaiana*) looks out in the morning, gauging whether it was warm enough to venture to a nearby patch of daisies (*Bellis sp.*). England.
Credit: Ed Phillips. (see page 2)

This book is for Rose, my love.

Contents

Introduction

There are more species of bees than birds and mammals combined. With at least 20,000 described species and with many new species being described annually, bees comprise a major component of our planet's biodiversity. They play a vital role in human ecology, a fact underlined by the estimate that every third mouthful of our food is dependent on the pollination services of bees.

Honeybees are the most intensively studied of all insects. Together with bumblebees and stingless bees, they are highly social. Such bees, though, account for only a very small proportion of the world's bee fauna. The vast majority of species, more than 90 percent, are solitary or non-social. Here, each nest is the work of a single female working alone; there is no caste of workers as in the highly social bees.

Nevertheless, most people are familiar with the social honeybees and bumblebees...but are they really? In television news items stock footage of bumblebees at flowers is used to illustrate pieces on colony collapse disorder in honeybees and, to even things up, footage of honeybees illustrates pieces on concern about declining populations of bumblebees. To add to the confusion, the iconography of labels on jars of honey often includes caricatures of bumblebees flying around a rustic-looking beehive!

Being social and making honey are in reality eccentric things for bees to be engaged in; the focus on social bees means that the vast majority of bees barely appear on the radar of public consciousness. One of the aims of this book, therefore, is to give due attention to the highly social bees and their importance in human affairs, but also to reset the balance and open up the solitary bees to a wider audience. These bees are highly diverse in terms of their nesting and mating behavior and their relationships with flowering plants.

In its broadest sense, biodiversity and its maintenance are now well and truly on the public agenda and, thanks to high quality natural history television documentaries, most of us are broadly familiar with the ecology of big game species in Africa. Only now, though, are we beginning to unravel the ecology of the little game, the insects, whose ecological services support and maintain habitats and ecosystems.

They do this via complex webs of interactions between themselves, plants and other organisms. These webs form a dynamic, self-sustaining safety net on which we depend and bees occupy keystone positions here. There is no doubt that visiting aliens from another galaxy would quickly realize that insects are the dominant terrestrial life forms on our planet rather than our own species.

This is important: our antecedents evolved in response to the opportunities and challenges presented by the savannahs of East Africa and they did so by courtesy of the ecological services provided by insects, including the bees, which continue to play vital roles in human ecology.

When early man migrated out of Africa, the habitats he encountered may have been different from those in Africa and the bees and plants were certainly different; nevertheless, the habitats he colonized were created and maintained by the same co-evolved, life-sustaining webs of bee-plant relationships.

It was only as late as the 18th century that people began to understand and value the pollination services of bees. This knowledge grew and developed in Britain and Europe and led to beehives being placed in fruit

A metallic green sweat bee *Agapostemon* sp. Credit: Jon Sullivan. (see page 6)

A male bumblebee, *Bombus vosnesenskii*, dusted with pollen, drinks nectar at a flower. Male bees do not collect pollen but they do contribute to pollination. California. Credit: Edward Ross. (opposite)

orchards specifically for pollination purposes and growers began to enjoy higher fruit yields.

Today, in the United States, bees pollinate 130 crop species and worldwide more than 400 crops. Most of this managed pollination is by honeybees and the value of these crops greatly exceeds the value of honey produced.

Honeybees, however, are now under increasing pressure from disease, parasites and the sinister colony collapse disorder. In the period 2009-2010, beekeepers in the United States lost on average 42.2 percent of their colonies and in the last 10-15 years, both the United States and Britain have lost nearly 50 percent of beekeepers, who have given up the craft. For too long we have relied on this single species as a managed pollinator.

If we are to recruit additional species, then we need to know more about the world's bees. Leafcutter bees (*Megachile* spp.) and mason bees (*Osmia* spp.) are some of the main contenders as alternative pollinators. The Alfalfa Leafcutter bee (*Megachile rotundata*) is managed on a large scale in Canada and the United States for pollination of alfalfa, an important forage crop for cattle. Bumblebees are now widely used in Britain, Europe and increasingly in the United States as pollinators of glasshouse crops, especially tomatoes and I have been involved in developing the management of the Eurasian Red Mason bee, *Osmia rufa* as an orchard pollinator and the Blue Orchard bee, *O. lignaria*, as a farmed pollinator of almonds in California and both species show great potential.

Many of our wild bee faunas, however, are already under threat from a variety of human activities, including increasing urbanization and the over-fragmentation of natural habitats, not to mention the reduced floral diversity associated with intensive agriculture. In the tropics, vast tracts of rain forest are being lost by logging and the ever-expanding palm oil industry. As E. O. Wilson, the great ant specialist and naturalist has put it, we run the risk of losing the book of life before we have finished reading the introduction.

Even where these bees are not actively managed, they still, in their "wild" state, make a valuable contribution to crop pollination. The vital role of bees in human ecology is underlined by the fact that much of the estimated third of human food dependent on bee pollination can be attributed to solitary bees.

The association of bees and man has thus been long and close. For me, it began as a 12 year-old, in the coastal sand dunes 24km (15 miles) north of Liverpool. It was here that I made my first discoveries about bees. Even now, as a full-grown man, give me a flower-rich meadow and a variety of pollen-plundering bees and I am as happy and excited as that boy in the Lancashire dunes. And there is much to be excited about.

Bees have an impressive diversity of size, form and nesting behavior. They can be found in high, alpine and sub-arctic regions, rainforest, savannahs, steppes and deserts. The greatest diversity of species occurs in shrub communities in regions with a Mediterranean-type climate: short, mild winters, warm springs and hot, dry summers.

Many species excavate nests in the ground, others construct exposed nests on rocks or vegetation while others nest in pre-existing cavities such as hollow plant stems, beetle borings in dead wood; some specialists use snail shells. Specialization is a theme running through this book—specialization in the nesting and foraging behavior of females and in the mate seeking behavior of males: all of the classic behaviors recorded in birds and mammals—scramble competition, lek displays and aggressive territoriality are also found among male bees.

We need bees, not only for the pollination of food crops, but also for the keystone roles they play in maintaining ecosystems and habitats, including many to which we accord aesthetic and recreational value.

Understanding the diversity of bees and their network of relationships with flowering plants is basic to any attempts to conserve many major habitats. Central to these challenges are considerations such as the size of, and distance between, fragmented reserves of natural habitat relative to the foraging distances of the bees that pollinate their floral components.

Bees: A Natural History

The Wasp
Inheritance

1

Plate 1–2

Plate 1–5

The Wasp Inheritance

relative to the nest/hive entrance. The bees perform a side-to-side figure-of-eight flight pattern immediately in from of the nest entrance. During this activity, they memorize near landmarks. These will be a mix of nearby structural features such as a prominent pebble, a twig and a patch of weed. My friend and colleague, Mark O'Neil has evidence that this behavior is switched on by emerging from a dark nest into the light at least in the case of bumblebees (*Bombus* species) and also that the navigation system is reset by this transition.

Gradually, the bee broadens the sweep of its flight pattern and increases its distance and height from the nest entrance. Now it is memorizing more distant landmarks and these may be features such as some prominent trees and rock outcrops. Finally, it increases its altitude even more and widens the breadth of its side-to-side flight pattern as it memorizes distant landmarks on the horizon. These may be a mountain peak, a row of pylons and/or a church steeple.

The bee is now ready to employ another landmark: the position of the sun relative to the nest entrance. This is called sun-compass orientation and may seem to us to be somewhat unreliable because the sun moves across the sky and its position may be obscured by clouds.

Bees, however, are not fooled by this. They have a built-in clock which accounts for the sun's movement. As for cloud cover, they know where the sun is, even if we can't see it: their eyes are sensitive to the plane of polarized light, so the position of the sun is not a mystery to them.

Integrating all this information requires some impressive on-board computing abilities. It enables bees to produce cognitive maps of their surroundings to such an extent that many species can forage many kilometers from their nests. (see Chapter 6)

Worker honeybees solve the traveling salesman's conundrum on a daily basis. That is, they work out the shortest route between all the patches of forage plants whose locations they have learned. Computers may take many hours to perform this feat.

Indeed, the processing of information by bees is a recurrent theme of this book. Not only can they orientate back to their nests over long distances, they assess the quality and distance from the nest of food and nest-building resources. Social bees also assess and act on their perceived needs of the colony.

Experiments have shown that a worker honeybee can learn that a particular scent at the entrance to a maze predicts which scent to follow to find a source of food. Without any further learning, the worker is able to apply the same rule but uses, instead, visual cues that it has never been exposed to in the maze. Thus, among many other things, bees can generalize.

All this processing is carried out with a brain which in most species is much smaller than a grain of rice. The honeybee brain is about the size of a sesame seed and has about 1,000,000 neurons; a human brain has 100 billion neurons.

When one considers the information processing feats of bees, there is no doubt that the typical bee has the computing power of a modern laptop, which means that it has a more powerful on-board computer than was available to NASA at the time of the moon landings. The Apollo Guidance Computer (AGP) had about the same computational capability as a first generation microcomputer of the early 1980's and it was a cubic meter or more of discrete logic and Transistor-Transistor Logic (TTL). More importantly it consumed tens of watts of power—the bee brain probably consumes milliwatts. One would expect it to be more powerful than the AGP: dynamic control of a non steady state unstable aero structure (the bee) requires a great deal of computational power.

It is small wonder, therefore, that research groups in both Europe and the United States are currently engaged in projects to produce a complete simulation of the worker honeybee brain. There is great potential for "Robobee" brains to control miniature drones or lead to the development of small scale super computers with very low power requirements. This would be of interest to many organizations, from intelligence services to the New York Stock Exchange; the latter's supercomputer occupies 9.8 acres (4ha).

Plate 1-6

Plate 1-6. The front and hind wings of all bees, including this honeybee, are held together in flight by a row of tiny hooks or hamuli on at the leading edge of the rear wing, which engages with a fold on the hind edge of the fore-wing. Credit: Charles Krebs.

Plate 2-1

The Business of Being a Bee

2

Bees have three suites of characters superimposed on the basic body plan of a crabronid wasp: specialized, branched body hairs to which pollen easily adheres, special structures for the handling and transport of pollen back to the nest and tongues longer than those of wasps, for the efficient gathering of nectar.

Anyone who has watched queen and worker bumblebees and worker honeybees foraging at flowers will be familiar with the pollen basket on each hind leg. The pollen basket or **corbiculum** comprises the shiny, slightly concave outer surface of the tibia of each hind leg. (Plates 4-5; 6-4; 6-6) There are usually two or three stiff, erect bristles on the smooth surface of the basket which support the growing pollen load and the bee adds a little nectar to the pollen too increase its adhesion to the basket.

Using a sequence of grooming movements, the worker passes pollen from the fore-leg to the middle leg, using dense patches of comb-like bristles on the underside of each. From there, the pollen is rasped on to a dense series of nine or ten rows of bristles on the inner face of the basitarsus of the hind leg. (Plate 1-1) The bee rubs the inner faces of both basitarsi together, an action which pushes the pollen upwards to the joint between the basitarsus and the tibia. A series of short, stout bristles acts as a rasp and moves the pollen onto the outer face of the tibia which forms the corbiculum. This final action has an interesting result: Pollen groomed by the right fore- and midlegs ends up on the left corbiculm and vice versa.

This series of complex and rapid pollen-grooming movements take place in flight or when hovering briefly after leaving the flower (see Plate 2-1), a remarkable piece of neuro-muscular co-ordination for such a tiny brain. It is rather like a man running on the spot and rolling a cigarette in each hand with outstretched arms.

Apart from honeybees, only female orchid bees and workers and queens of bumblebees and stingless honeybees have pollen baskets or corbiculae. Collectively, these bees are sometimes referred to as the **corbiculate** bees and they form only about 4 percent of the 20,000+ bee species.

The pollen transport structures of the remaining bees comprise brushes of specialized hairs. With the exception of one bee family, the brush or **scopa** is situated, like the corbiculum, on the outer surface of the tibia of the hind leg; in species of the mining bee species *Andrena*, there is an additional scopa on the femur and some *Andrena* have a form of pollen basket on the sides of the propodeum.

The exceptions to leg-based pollen transport structures are females of the leafcutter, mason and carder bees (Family: Megachilidae, see below), where the scopa comprises dense tracts of specialized hairs on the underside of the abdomen.

Bees capitalized on their inheritance of sucking mouthparts by evolving longer tongues, enabling them to exploit tubular flowers. Some bees even have specialized tongues for the harvesting of pollen. They visit deep, narrow, tubular flowers in which the pollen bearing anthers cannot be reached by the front legs. (see Chapter 7)

The various ways in which bees transport pollen back to the nest are of interest to entomologists, particularly those of us who study the classification of bees. They provide some of the structural features which contribute diagnostic characters upon which the classification of bees is based: the naming of parts contributes to the naming of bees.

Plate 2-1. A worker Western Honeybee, *Apis mellifera*, hovers in over a flower, transferring pollen from the mid-leg to the hind leg. Credit: Edward Ross. (see page 24)

The branch of biology concerned with classification is called **taxonomy.** A good classification aspires to reflect evolutionary history and the basic unit here, is the species. A species is defined as a population of interbreeding individuals which produces viable offspring and does not normally seek to mate with members of any other species. Some species, such as our own, have a global distribution, others are restricted to a continent or a region within a continent; others may be restricted to highly specialized habitats. A good example is the large mites which live exclusively in special pouches in the abdomens of some large carpenter bees. (see Chapter 9)

Something like this species concept was evolving during the 18th century and a Swedish botanist, Carl von Linné, devised a system of naming plants and animals in a systematic way. More usually referred to by the Latinized form of his name, Carolus Linnaeus, his *Systema Naturae*, published in 1756, was timely. Natural history was a growing hobby among the leisured classes of Europe whose instinct to collect fossils, plants and animals reached its peak in the 19th Century with the Gentleman's Cabinet of Curiosities, a feature of many drawing rooms and studies. Despite many changes, his basic system, outlined in the 10th (1758) edition of his great work, is still used for naming, ranking and classifying organisms today.

One of the most important results of his system involved the use of Latin or Greek names for species. When English settlers arrived in North America from Europe in the 1600's, they found a common bird with a red breast. They called it the Robin or Robin Redbreast, after a bird they had left behind in the old country. Unfortunately, the European Robin and the American Robin are not only very different species; they belong to different families. The European Robin belongs to the family that comprises the Old World Flycatchers (Muscicapidae) and the North American Robin is a thrush (Turdidae).

The moral of this story is that any classification using common or vernacular names is intrinsically unstable because the names vary with geography and language.

The widespread acceptance of Linnaeus's neat system of naming organisms began to eliminate such complications. It established stability at a time when explorers and colonial administrators began to sample the huge diversity of living things. It is now called the binomial system because each species has two names: the genus or generic name and the species name. The initial letter of a generic name is always capitalized, that of the species is not. Thus, our own species is in the genus *Homo*, and we belong to the species *sapiens*. Generic and specific names are always printed in italics.

The use of these names means that when I visit a museum for research purposes in a country whose language I do not speak, I can use the universally recognized names of the bees I wish to see and I am understood immediately. With insects, there are so many species that there is simply no hope of each one having its own common name. This is the reason why this book is peppered with so many scientific names.

A genus comprises a group of species which are more closely related to each other than to any other species. And a family is a group of genera which are more closely related to each other than any other genera and so-on. In other words, each ranking comprises a nested set of categories. Table 1 outlines the full hierarchy of ranked names and categories for the Western Honeybee and our own species.

Table 2-1. A comparative classification of the Western Honeybee, *Apis mellifera* and humans, *Homo sapiens*.

Category	Western Honeybee	Humans
Kingdom	Animalia	Animalia
Phylum	Arthropoda: Jointed-limbed invertebrates: crabs, lobsters, centipedes, millipedes, spiders	Chordata: animals with a backbone
Class	Insecta: insects	Mammalia: warm-blooded hairy animals which suckle their young
Order	Hymenoptera: sawflies, horntails, ants, wasps, bees	Primates: monkeys and apes
Family	Apidae: solitary long-tongued bees with pollen scopae; social long-tongued bees with corbiculae	Hominidae: Great apes; humans
Subfamily	Apinae: bees with pollen baskets (corbiculae): orchid bees, bumblebees, stingless honeybees, true honeybees	Homininae: Gorillas, chimpanzees, bonobos, humans
Tribe	Apini: true honeybees	Hominini: Chimpanzees, bonobos, humans
Genus	*Apis*: 11 species of honeybee	*Homo*: humans, including fossil species
Species	*mellifera*: Western Honeybee	*sapiens*: modern humans

Note that tribal, subfamily and family names always end in the letters ...ini, ...inae and ...idae respectively, for all groups of animals. Flowering plant families end in ...aceae. The adjectives derived from family names end in ...id. Thus apid for Apidae.

Plate 2-2. A cladogram of the seven bee families. Here, the hunting wasp family is depicted as the sister group of the bees, however, recent molecular studies suggest the intriguing idea that the bees may have evolved within the family Crabronidae. Credit: Modified, with permission, from an original by Bryan Danforth.

Phylogeny of the bee families

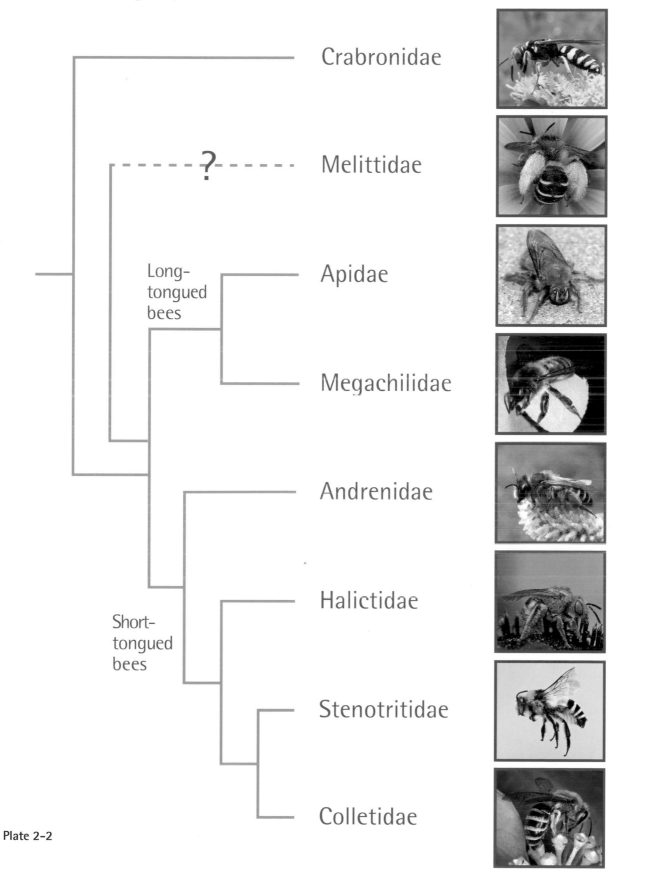

Crabronidae

? Melittidae

Long-tongued bees

Apidae

Megachilidae

Andrenidae

Short-tongued bees

Halictidae

Stenotritidae

Colletidae

Plate 2-2

Plate 2–3

30 Bees: A Natural History

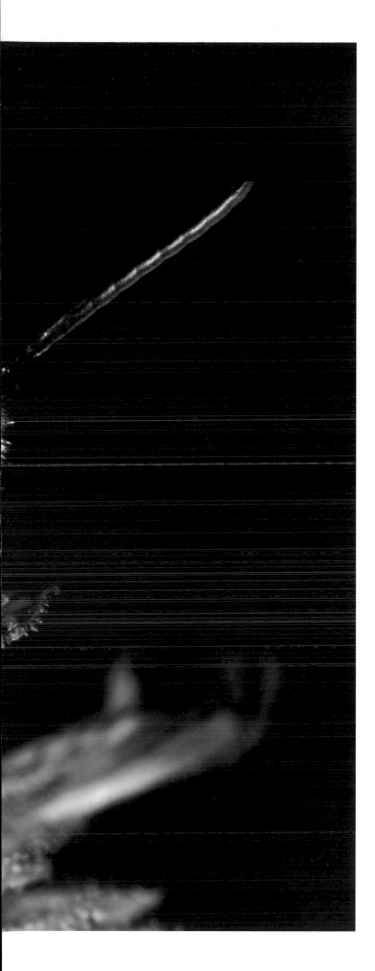

The use of scientific names for plants and animals is not a guild practice restricted to biologists. Gardeners are familiar with their use and my 37 years of experience working in the Oxford University Museum of Natural History taught me that school children interested in dinosaurs love them: they would visit the museum and ask for *Tyrannosaurus rex* and *Diplodocus carnegii* by name.

Having a universally accepted system of naming living things is of great practical value and importance outside the arcane world of taxonomy. Ecological surveys and biodiversity studies need accurately named species, as do people dealing with insects of medical, forensic and agricultural importance.

Hunter-gatherer societies are always expert taxonomists of the plants and animals important to their survival. Indeed, despite claims from certain quarters, taxonomy is the oldest of professions, having divine sanction recorded in the Book of Genesis, where, it is alleged, God instructed Adam to name all the creatures of the world.

Whether a hunter-gatherer or an entomologist, the taxonomist studies and systematizes structural and behavioral features in order to assemble a suite of characters which typify or define a species. For the hunter-gatherer, this has predictive and survival value in the field. For the taxonomist, this provides a means of identifying a species and distinguishing it from other, related species. The entomological taxonomist has higher aspirations: he or she seeks to produce identification keys which facilitate the work of ecologists, medical and agricultural entomologists. Another aspiration is to develop classifications that reflect the evolutionary history of the target group.

For insects, the structural characters are varied and mostly microscopic. For bees in particular, they include details of the surface sculpturing of the cuticle, the color and distribution of often specialized hairs,

Plate 2-3. A desert mining bee, *Centris* sp. drinks nectar in Tanque Verde Canyon, Arizona. Credit: Jillian H. Cowles.

Plate 2-4

Plate 2-4. Size range within a colony
of the bumblebee, *Bombus huntii.*
An overwintered queen is on the left.
Credit: Whitney Cranshaw.

Bees: A Natural History

the relative proportions of body parts, the color of both cuticle and hairs and much, much more.

The hard parts of genitalia of male insects are almost always diagnostic at the species level and in bees this also true of the hidden, highly modified segments of the abdomen, or metasoma, associated with the genitalia.

Behavioral traits, for example, nesting behavior and specialized relationships with flowering plants, can complement information from structural features. The same is true for more recent developments in molecular studies. Very often, molecular studies can resolve ambiguities in classifications based largely on structural features.

Evidence from comparative anatomy and recent molecular studies provide strong support for hypothesis that the hunting wasp family, Crabronidae, is the closest relative of the bees. This large family is still extant and is widespread, with more than 9000 species. (see Plate 1-2 page)

Plate 2-2 outlines the relationship of bees with the crabronid wasps, together with current views of the relationships between the seven families of bees. This is not a family tree in the sense of genealogists, but a diagrammatic representation called a cladogram, the result of an analytical approach to classification called cladistics.

This particular cladogram is based on the family ranking. Within each depicted family, there can be cladograms for relationships between the genera or species comprising the family. Similarly, there can be cladograms for rankings above the family.

Whatever the ranking, the basic tenet of the cladistic approach is that each branch is a group with shared, derived (= advanced) characters that are not shared with any other groups, for example, the honeybee family Apidae. Its nearest neighboring group, termed **sister** group, the Megachilidae, shares derived characters with the Apidae that neither shares with any other group. In other words, they have a more recent, common ancestor than either has with any other family. Each level in the taxonomic hierarchy is defined by a unique set of nested, derived characters.

Cladograms of this sort are best regarded as works in progress; perceived relationships may change with the discovery of new species or revised analyses or interpretations of structural and/or molecular data.

Plate 2-5

Bees: A Natural History

Plate 2-5. A Western Honeybee, *Apis mellifera*, covered in the very large pollen grains of a pumpkin flower, *Cucurbita cultivar*. These pollen grains are probably too large for the pollen handling structures of honeybees to build up a full load in their pollen baskets. Italy. Credit: John Kimbler/ Tom Stack and Associates.

The Families of bees

The genera cited under the following bee families are, for the most part, those most likely to be encountered by the general reader in North, Central and South America and Eurasia, but this is in no way a complete outline. African and Australasian genera of note are cited where appropriate.

Melittidae

A small family of solitary mining bees, most species being associated with dry climates. The principal genera are *Dasypoda*, (Eurasia) (see Plate 3-5); *Hesperapis* (North America and South Africa); *Melitta* (North America, Eurasia and South Africa); *Rediviva* (southern Africa) (see Plates 7-3, 8-4) and *Macropis* (North America and Eurasia). (Plate 2-3) The scopae of *Dasypoda* are massively developed. Females of *Macropis* and *Rediviva* collect floral oils.

Apidae

A large and diverse family of long-tongued bees, divisible into two major groups: those which have scopae on the hind legs for the transport of pollen and the so-called corbiculate bees, which transport pollen in a pollen basket or corbiculum on the hind leg (Plate 6-4). Behaviorally, they range from solitary to highly social species.

The principal solitary genera with pollen scopae include: *Xylocopa,* the Giant Carpenter bees (All continents) (Plate 4-3); *Ceratina* (All continents); and *Allodape* and related genera, the dwarf carpenter bees (Africa, Asia, Australia). The Giant Carpenter bees excavate nests in solid wood, with the exception of 16 · species, which nest in the ground and some of which are crepuscular and nocturnal. The dwarf carpenter bees excavate nests in pithy stems.

The following genera with pollen scopae all nest in the ground: *Diadasia* (North and South America); Long-horned bees (Eucerini), so-called because the males have extremely long antennae, often reaching back to just beyond the base of the abdomen: *Peponapis* (see Plate 7-1) and *Melissodes* (North and South America); *Xenoglossa,* (North America); *Eucera,* (Plate 5-2; 6-7; and 8-8); and *Tetraloniella* (North America, Eurasia).

Other genera with many species which nest in the ground are *Anthophora,* (North America, Africa, and Eurasia) (see Plates 1-3, 3-2, 3-3, 3-6, 5-1, 5-4) *Amegilla* (Africa, Eurasia, and Australia) (see Plates 6-8 and 10-5) and *Centris* (North and South America) (Plate 2-6).

Apart from the genera listed above, there are many apids which are cuckoo bees, that is, they lay eggs in the nests of other species. (see Chapter 9)

Plate 2-6. A male resin bee, *Megachile nigrovittata.* The females of this Australian bee are unusual for Megachile in using resin collected from plants as a building material rather than cut pieces of leaf.
Credit: Laurence Sanders

Plate 2-6

The remaining Apidae are the corbiculate bees: the Orchid bees (Euglossini): *Eufriesea, Euglossa* (see Plates 4-2 and 8-6), and *Eulaema* (Plate 8-4). Orchid bees are found in the tropical forests of Central and South America. One species, *Euglossa viridissima* has become established in Florida. Two genera, *Aglae* and *Exaerete*, are cuckoos in the nests of other orchid bees and the females lack corbiculae.

Bumblebees (*Bombus* spp.) are found in North and South America, North Africa and Eurasia. (Plate 2-4 and 4-5) Some species are adapted to life at high altitude, others at high latitudes, above the Arctic Circle. The species comprising the subgenus *Psithyrus* are cuckoos in the nests of other species of *Bombus*.

The stingless honeybees live in both the Old World and New World tropics and subtropics. The principal genera are *Melipona* (Central and South America) and *Trigona* (Central and South America, Asia and Australia). Several stingless bee genera are robbers or cuckoos in the nests of other stingless bees. (see Chapter 9)

The true honeybees comprise the genus *Apis*. There are eleven species. The Western Honeybee (*Apis mellifera*) native to Western Europe and sub-Saharan Africa is the species most widely used for honey production and as a managed pollinator. (see Plates 1-1, 1-5, 2-1, 2-5) It was introduced to North America by early European settlers, where the Native Americans called it "the white man's fly."

Plate 2-7. A female solitary mining bee, *Andrena flavipes*. Like many spring bees, this solitary andrenid mining bee forages at willow catkins, *Salix* spp. England. Credit: Nigel Jones.

Bees: A Natural History

Plate 2-7

The Business of Being a Bee

Plate 2-8

Megachilidae

This family comprises the other group of long-tongued bees. They differ from all other bee families in having the pollen scopa on the underside of the abdomen. They use collected materials rather than glandular secretions to line and seal brood cells and the majority nest in pre-existing cavities; some build nests above ground and a few nest underground.

The principal genera are *Megachile* (Plate 2-6 and 3-8), the leaf-cutter bees found on all continents; and the mason bees, *Osmia* (Plates 3-7; 10-3; 10-6; and 14-4) (North America and Eurasia), *Hoplitis, Heriades, Chelostoma* (North America and Eurasia), and *Ashmeadiella.*

Species of *Anthidium* (North America and Eurasia) are called carder bees because of the habit of stripping plant hairs for use as a nest building material. (Plates 3-11 and Plate 5-5)

Andrenidae

This and the remaining families are short-tongued bees. The Andrenidae excavate nests in the ground and occur on all continents except Australia. *Andrena* is the principal genus in temperate climates of the Northern Hemisphere, with more than one thousand described species. (Plates 2-7 and 4-1).

Calliopsis and *Perdita* (Plate 2-8) species are restricted to North America, with *Panurginus* found in North America and Eurasia, while *Panurgus* occurs in Eurasia.

Plate 2-8. Diversity in size. One of the world's tiniest of bees, a female andrenid mining bee, *Perdita minima*, on the head of a female giant carpenter bee, *Xylocopa* sp, North America. The scale bar = 1mm. Credit: Steve Buchman.

Halictidae

These mining bees are often called sweat bees because of their attraction to human sweat. The family is very large, with many species and genera. Many are metallic blue or green in color and some are social. (see Chapter 4) The principal genera are *Halictus* and *Lasioglossum* (North America and Eurasia; Plate 4-4); *Agapostemon* (see contents page) and *Augochloropsis* (Plate 6-2) both genera found in North and South America; and *Nomia* (North America, Africa, Eurasia and Australia) (Plate 2-7).

Stenotritidae

This mining bee family is restricted to Australia and has just two genera, *Stenotritus* (11 spp.) and *Ctenocolletes*, (10 spp).

Colletidae

Colletes is the most widespread genus of this mining bee family and occurs on all continents except Australia. (Plates 2-10)

The species-rich genus *Hylaeus* occurs on all continents and is divided into many subgenera. Most species nest in pithy stems rather than the ground and some nest in pre-existing cavities such as beetle borings in wood or plant galls. Many species are found on islands. Female *Hylaeus* do not have a pollen scopa on their legs. Instead, they transport pollen in the crop, along with nectar.

Plate 2-9. A male *Nomia* sp. Huachuca Mountains, Cochise County, Arizona. Credit: Jillian H. Cowles.

Plate 2-9

Plate 2–10

Plate 2–10 A female Ivy bee, *Colletes hederae*, at an ivy flower, *Hedera* helix, autumn, Dorset, England. Credit: Peter O'Toole.

Plate 3–1

Solitary Bees

3

The vast majority of the world's bees are solitary species. That is, they do not live in colonies like bumblebees or honeybees. Instead, each nest is the work of a single female working alone and there is no worker caste. There is no overlap of generations, so a female dies before her offspring become adult.

The solitary life-style does not, however, always mean small or sparse populations: many solitary species often nest in dense aggregations and in such large numbers as to attract human attention.

While solitary bees have a diverse range of nesting behaviors, they share a number of traits. The females of all species construct a space, the brood cell, in which they store pollen, usually mixed with some nectar. When the provision is complete, the female usually lays a single egg on the food store. Some species lay the egg on the side of the cell.

Most species in temperate regions have a single generation per year. They are said to be **univoltine**. A minority have two (**bivoltine**). Notable exceptions are mining bee species of the apid mining bee genus *Amegilla*, which in Mediterranean and other dry regions have several generations per year and are termed multivoltine. Bivoltine and multivoltine species are more frequent in the tropics.

In temperate regions, the offspring of species which are active in early spring become adult in their natal cells in late summer or early autumn.

Plate 3-1. A male of the widespread Eurasian mason bee, *Osmia caerulescens*. The thousands of facets (ommatidia) making up the compound eye are clearly visible. Naples, Italy. Credit: John Kimbler. (see page 46)

Plate 3-2. A female of the common North American apid mining bee, *Anthophora bomboides*, hovering at her nest entrance, possibly making an orientation flight. Credit: Kathy Keatley Garvey.

Bees: A Natural History

Plate 3-2

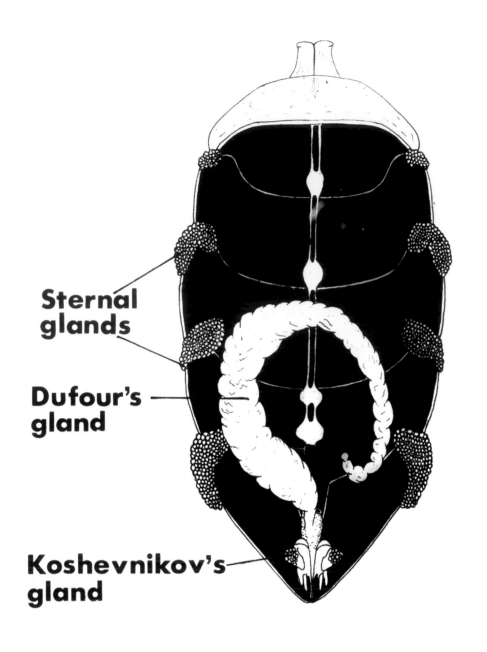

Sternal glands

Dufour's gland

Koshevnikov's gland

Plate 3-3

Plate 3-3. (left) A dissected abdomen of a female colletid mining bee, *Colletes cunicularius*, showing the Dufour's gland, the source of the nest lining material. (above) The tip of the abdomen of the apid mining bee, *Anthophora hermanni*, showing the triangular pygidial plate, used to apply the cell lining substance from the Dufour's gland. Credit: Christopher O'Toole.

In contrast, the offspring of species which are active in summer overwinter as prepupae. They then pupate the following springs and emerge as adults in summer.

For the females of most solitary bees, life can be summarized as a sequence of behaviors, the completion of one being the stimulus for the next:

Emergence > mating > searching for nest-site > nest construction > foraging to provision > 1st brood cell > laying single egg > sealing of cell > construction of 2nd brood cell and so on until sealing of completed nest.

All these activities are fuelled by frequent visits to flowers in order to feed on energy-rich nectar.

Mining bees

Mining bees are so-called because they excavate nests in the ground. Some species prefer to nest in sand, others in light, sandy loams; others prefer clay soils. Many nest in flat ground, often in hard pan such as the apid mining bee *Anthophora romandii* in North Africa and the deserts of the Middle East. Others use inclined banks and some often use cliff faces, such as the North American apid mining bee, *Anthophora bomboides* (Plate 3-6) and the Eurasian Hairy-footed Flower bee, *A. plumipes.* (see Plate 3-7)

The nests of mining bees show a wide range of subterranean architecture, but almost all comprise a main tunnel with side branches, with a single brood cell at the end of each branch.

Plate 3-4. (top) A single, transparent brood cell of a North American plasterer bee, *Colletes validus*, showing the semiliquid pollen-nectar mixtures and a single egg attached to the cell wall. Credit: Jim Cane; (bottom) A section through a brood cell of the Alkali bee, *Nomia melanderi*, showing the smooth cell lining and the molded pollen mass, with a young larva. Marin Co., California. Credit: Edward Ross.

Nesting in the ground has its hazards: soils can become very damp or waterlogged. With such conditions there is a danger of mould destroying both pollen stores and developing bees. However, almost all mining bees have evolved a solution to this by applying waterproof and fungus-resistant linings to brood cells. The linings are secretions from the Dufour's gland, which empties into the sting chamber. This is the largest abdominal structure in female mining bees. (Plate 3-3)

I first realized the water-proofing efficiency of cell linings when in winter I once drove past the site of a large, isolated, dense nesting aggregation of a species of plasterer bee, *Colletes succinctus*, which I had studied for several years. The nests were in the banks of a river, which, I discovered, was frequently flooded in winter. The following summer, the bees were active as normal. In North America, the Swamp Sand bee (*Perdita floridensis*), a sand-nesting andrenid is also seasonally aquatic in the same way.

Female plasterer bees, *Colletes* spp., produce a transparent, cellophane-like cell lining. (Plate 3-4)

The bee applies it in liquid form, using her short, blunt tongue as a kind of paint brush. The secretion is primarily a mixture of chemicals called macrocyclic lactones which polymerize when applied to the cell wall, forming a natural polyester. The lining dries and is not incorporated into the sand and is easily separated from it. Until recently, the tongue of colletid bees was referred to as "wasp-like" and taken to indicate the primitive nature of this group. It is, however, now regarded as a derived or advanced feature, an adaptation for the application of Dufour's gland secretion to cell walls.

Mining bees in the family Halictidae, the so-called sweat bees, also line their brood cells with a mixture of macrocyclic lactones. Unlike *Colletes*, though, halictids produce the lactones in a form which is waxy, smooth and is incorporated into the soil. (see Plate 3-4 right)

Short-tongued (Andrenidae) and Long-tongued (Anthophoridae) mining bees also produce cell linings with a waxy finish and which are incorporated into the soil, though they are chemically very different from

Plate 3-4

Solitary Bees

lactones. For example, the Dufour's gland secretion of *Anthophora* species is a mixture of fatty compounds called triglycerides. As well as using these for cell lining purposes, female *Anthophora* mix the triglycerides with the stored pollen as an additional food for the larvae.

Only plasterer bees, *Colletes* spp., use their tongues to apply Dufour's gland secretion to cell walls. Others, such as the many species of *Andrena* and anthophorid genera such as *Eucera*, *Anthophora* and relatives, have a raised triangular area at the apex of the abdomen. This is called the **pygidium**, which functions rather like a plasterer's trowel. (see Plate 3-3)

Taken across the families of bees, Dufour's gland produces a wide range of cell lining substances. This chemical diversity suggests the independent evolution of different chemical pathways, all resulting in finished products with the same two vital, functional properties: waterproofing and resistance to fungal and bacterial attack. Being waterproof also protects food stores and larvae from desiccation in arid areas.

The secretions of this remarkable gland also have other functions. Some species use it as an individual nest marking scent and it is believed that it has a sexual function in others.

Curiously, the females of the Eurasian melittid mining bee genus, *Dasypoda* (see Plate 3-5), do not produce a cell lining. They nest in dry, sandy habitats and have an adaptation thought to minimize the infiltration of the pollen mass by mould. The pollen mass is sculpted so that it stands on a tripod to reduce the amount of contact between pollen and cell wall.

Many mining bee species nest in dense aggregations comprising hundreds to many thousands of nests. Just why they do this is not always clear but with the North American halictid, the alkali bee (*Nomia melanderi*) it has been shown that it needs alkaline soils which are damp beneath a surface crust. Such conditions can be patchy in distribution, leading to the build up of nesting populations, which is fortunate for alfalfa growers because this bee is an important pollinator of this crop. (see Chapter 10)

In the Negev Desert, Israel, I found populations of the apid mining bee, *Anthophora romandii*, excavating nests in dense aggregations in hard pan between sand dunes. This is a remarkable species because the hard pan is really hard and requires persistent biting with their mandibles to make any impression. Each female builds a turret above the nest entrance made of loose spoil from her digging activities (Plate 3-6). The bees use saliva to soften the building materials. Given that they live in a harsh desert environment, there must be a good reason for investing time, energy and scarce water resources in this way. The temperature was 42°C (107°F) and there were no forage plants visible in the near vicinity.

I noticed that when returning to their nests, females usually antennated the rim of their nest turrets, suggesting that they may be identifying their nests by scent, a common behavior in mining bees. While observing this it became obvious that excavated spoil was often moved around by regular, small-scale dust devils, and drifted up against the nest turrets.

Perhaps the construction of turrets was an adaptation to prevent wind-blown spoil from in-filling the nest entrance. To test this, I removed the turrets from five nests and waited to see what happened. Spoil had completely obscured the nest entrance of two of the nests; in the remaining three, it had blown into them and accumulated just below the entrance without obscuring it. The females returning to these had no difficulty in recognizing their nests: they antennated the nest entrance, suggesting that, if scent was involved in individual nest recognition, it was also

Plate 3-5. A female Eurasian melittid mining bee, *Dasypoda hirtipes*, at her nest entrance. Note the massively developed pollen scopa on each hind leg. Credit: Arie Koster.

Plate 3-5

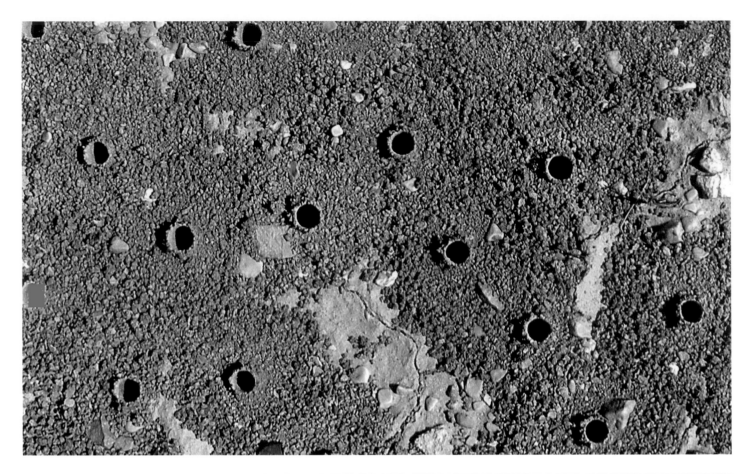

Plate 3–6

Bees: A Natural History

deposited on the sides of the nest tunnel, below the level of the turret.

Two of the females excavated the in-fill, each taking about five minutes; in so doing, much of the pollen load was abraded from their scopae. They then proceeded to reconstruct their turrets. The third also removed the in-fill and then disappeared into the nest.

The females whose nests were completely obscured by the wind-blown soil landed close to them, antennating the surface. This hints that visual cues led them to the close vicinity of their nests, but they were unable to find the entrances. They spent time running about near to the invisible nests, then started investigating open, neighboring nests and disappeared inside them.

It seems, then, that in this situation, turrets give some protection from inundation by wind-blown spoil. The turrets are just high enough not to be inundated, thus saving returning bees expenditure of time, energy and lost pollen in removing debris. The bees are thus adapted to balance their resources in ways appropriate to living on the edge in an extreme environment.

The ability of large species of *Anthophora* to dig nests in hard substrates can be important for other, smaller bees. I was able to observe this in the *wadis* of the Negev Desert, Israel. I found three species of *Anthophora*—*fulvitarsis, agama,* and *senescens*—nesting in mixed species aggregations along the vertical cliffs forming the sides of Wadi Loz. Many generations of nesting activity have caused erosion, resulting in partial exposure of sections of old nest tunnels and cells; a smaller relation of the *Anthophora, Heliophila*

lutulenta, and several as yet unidentified mason bees nested secondarily in the old nest structures of the larger bees.

The nesting activities of the large bees had resulted in a build-up of a bank of fine, semi-compacted soil along the bottom of the cliff. This provides a nest site for bees which are too small to be able to burrow into the hard, sun-baked cliff face. These included a small species of the andrenid genus *Panurginus*, a tiny halictid, *Nomioides* sp., and another halictid, a sweat bee, *Lasioglossum* sp.

The small, short-tongued bees forage at small, open access flowers which grow along the bottom of the *wadi*. The large bees ignore these. Instead, females of the four *Anthophora* species nesting in the cliff mostly flew directly out of their nests and over a hill; they are long-tongued, long distance pollinators and there were few long-tubed flowers in the *wadi*. It is clear that in Wadi Loz, at least, there is an intriguing pollination network, based on the availability of nest sites: the reproductive success of the small flowers in the wadi may well depend on the nesting success of large bees which never visit them.

An Eurasian mining bee, *Andrena vetula*, is another species which nests in dense aggregations. It is unusual that it nests in the floors of caves, in the twilight zone, far enough in for the human eye to need some time to accommodate to the gloom. I first encountered this bee in the Kebara Cave in the Carmel Massif in Israel. This limestone cave is famous for the discovery there of "Mt. Carmel Man," one of the most complete Neanderthal skeletons. I subsequently found populations of this bee nesting in several old Roman tombs carved out of friable beachrock along the coastal plain of Israel.

The cave-nesting habits of this bee have resulted in two distinct mate-searching strategies by the males. (see Chapter 5)

The Kebara Cave was shared with another bee, the Hairy-footed mining bee, *Anthophora plumipes*, whose small nesting aggregations were high up in the wall of the cave between wet seepages. The nests were in almost complete darkness. The species also had

Plate 3-6. (top) Part of a huge nest aggregation of the apid mining bee, *Anthophora romandii*. The species nests in hard pan between desert dunes and the females build short turrets which prevent the loose spoil from their excavations blocking their nest entrances. (bottom) A female *Anthophora romandii* adds excavated soil to her nest entrance turret. Negev Desert, Israel. Credit: Christopher O'Toole.

a nesting population in the soft plaster and mortar in the cells of a ruined Turkish prison, deep in the Carmel Forest.

Anthophora plumipes is remarkable for another reason: it lives in a wide range of climatic zones. Its distribution extends from Britain (including my garden in Leicestershire), across Northern Europe and around the Mediterranean, the Middle East, including the Judean and Negev Deserts, through central Asia and to Japan. It has now been introduced and become established in the eastern United States.

The dense nesting aggregations of mining bees often have strong, characteristic smells. These scents are produced by glands at the base of the mandibles and both sexes emit them. Sometimes one has to get down and close to the nests to appreciate this, but this is not necessary with dense nesting populations of plasterer bees (*Colletes* spp.). Their mandibular gland scent is linalool and a dense nesting population smells very strongly of this attractive substance. Linalool belongs to a class of volatile chemicals called terpenes and it is the major component in all species of *Colletes* whose mandibular gland scents been have been studied. Some species of *Colletes* also secrete geraniol and neral together with linalool. In *Colletes*, linalool has a triple function. It is a sex pheromone (see Chapter 5), an aggregation pheromone which attracts males and females to an established nesting population and an anti-bacterial and fungal agent, which a female emits around the entrance to a completed cell and just before she seals it.

I exploited the aggregation pheromone function of linalool during my involvement in the making of a film on solitary bees for television. We wanted to film a strong, dense aggregation of *Colletes cunicularius* and I needed to find one in a very large area of coastal dunes in South Wales. I smeared linalool over my beard and hair and walked through the seaward area of the dunes, with the onshore wind carrying the smell of linalool into the dunes. Within a few minutes I had males flying up the vapor plume towards me and flying around my head, occasionally landing in my hair and beard. I followed the direction the bees were coming from and eventually found three areas with the beginning of nesting activity. Females were just emerging and there were large numbers of males cruising low over the ground in search of mates.

I was not unique in anointing myself with this sweet component of lavender oil. Linalool, together with the sexual scents of other bees and flowers, are now part of the recent natural history of our own species. We scrupulously remove our own sexual scents and the hair tufts which act as dispersal wicks and replace them with the synthesized sexual scents of other species in deodorants and antiperspirants. Linalool, geranial and limonene are widespread in a wide range of cosmetics, toothpaste, liquid detergents and fabric conditioners. Geraniol has also been used as a flavor enhancer of cigarettes and linalool is also used as such in bilberry yogurt.

Plate 3-7. A female snail-nesting mason bee, *Osmia cinnabarina*, at her nest. Credit: Nico J. Vereecken.

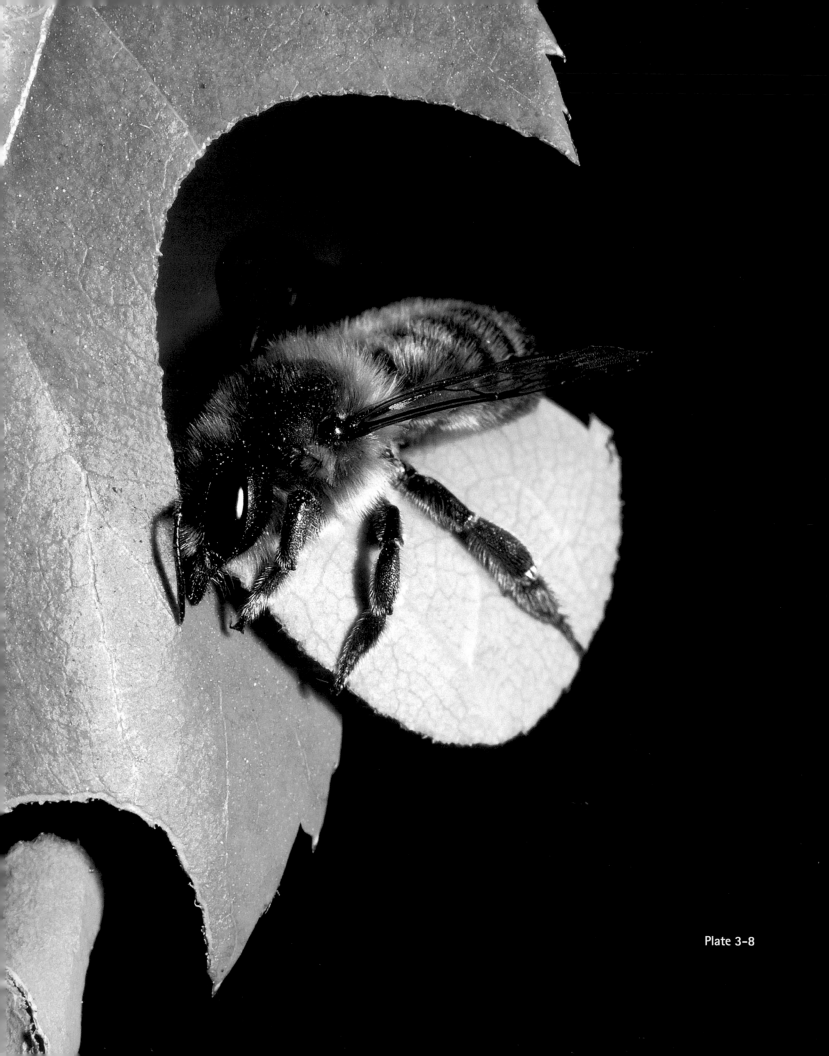

Plate 3-8

Leafcutter, Mason, Carder and Carpenter Bees: Cavity and surface-nesters

With the exception of the carpenter bees, mason bees, leafcutters, and carder bees belong to the family Megachilidae. This means that they differ from the mining bee families in having the pollen scopa on the underside of the abdomen.

They differ, too, in their nesting habits. The majority of megachilids nest in pre-existing cavities such as hollow plant stems or beetle borings in dead wood. Some nest also in pithy stems, others build exposed nests on rocks or plant stems and only a few excavate nests in the ground. A few mason bees nest exclusively in empty snail shells. (Plate 3-7)

Megachilids do not use Dufour's gland secretions to line and seal their cells. Instead, according to species, they collect materials such as leaf pieces, mud and resin or make a mastic of finely chewed leaf pieces. These bees also differ from mining bees in that their pre-pupae spin a tough silk cocoon prior to pupation.

Leafcutter bees

Leafcutter bees comprise the genus *Megachile*. Females line their nests with pieces of cut leaf which they excise from leaf margins using their powerful jaws. (Plate 3-8; and see film of a female *Megachile relativa* constructing her nest cells at http://www.youtube.com/watch?v=EjsZ419ImMY)

Depending on the size of the *Megachile* species, the lining of each cell comprises 10–25 pieces of leaf, each slightly different in shape so as to fit together to make a cylinder. Females seal each cell and their completed nests with a series of perfectly circular leaf discs. The bees use a salivary secretion to glue together all the leaf pieces.

Unlike most mining bees, leafcutter bees do not mould their pollen stores into near perfect spheres. Instead, they store pollen in a mass at the rear of the cell. They mix nectar with the pollen, giving it a syrupy consistency. In at least some species, the Dufour's gland is enlarged as in mining bees and the females mix the secretion from this with the pollen-nectar mass.

Megachile species occur in all the major continents; there are 53 subgenera and several hundred species, one of which, the Alfalfa Leafcutter bee (*M. rotundata*) has already been used as an alfalfa pollinator in Canada, the United States and Chile for many years (see Chapter 10) and several more have this potential.

Plate 3-8. A female leafcutter bee, *Megachile willughbiella*, cuts a piece of leaf from a rose which with to line her nest. Credit: Ken Preston-Mafham/Prema Photos Wildlife.

Mason bees are so-called because they collect pliable material which they use for nest construction. According to species, these materials are mud, small pebbles mixed with mud, resin or a mastic of finely chewed leaves mixed with saliva. Some species nest secondarily in the empty cells of mud-dauber wasps and a few nest in the ground, lining their cells with petals and sealing them with a mixture of sand and saliva.

Some species of *Megachile* (subgenus *Chalicodoma*) and a Eurasian Mason bee, *Hoplitis anthocopoides*, make exposed mud nests on cliff faces or rocks. Nests of the latter comprise clusters of cells made of small pebbles cemented together with mud.

The longest bee in the world, 39mm (1.53 inches) is Wallace's Giant Mason bee, *Megachile pluto.* (Plate 3-9) It has a wingspan of 63mm (2.5 inches) and is notable for its huge, elongate mandibles. It was collected on the island of Bacan (Bachian) in the Malay Archipelago in 1859 by the great Victorian naturalist Alfred Russell Wallace. For 122 years this bee was known only from the single type specimen in the Oxford University Museum of Natural History, where I had the pleasure of curating it for 37 years. Nothing was known of its nesting biology, then, in 1981, an American biologist, Adam Messer found a total of six nests on Bacan and nearby islands.

Messer found that the bee burrows in the sides of active nests of a termite, *Microcerotermes* spp. The termites use chewed wood fibers as a building material, nesting on tree trunks and branches. Apart from being digging tools, female *Megachile pluto* also use their massive jaws to create resin flows by wounding trees. The bee then uses back and forward movements of its head to build up a ball of resin about

Plate 3-9. The female type specimen of Wallace's Giant Mason bee, *Megachile (Chalicodoma) pluto*, Collected by Alfred Russell Wallace in 1859 on the island of Bacan in the Malay Archipelago. Credit: Hope Entomological Collections, Oxford University Museum of Natural History.

Plate 3-9

Plate 3-10

64

10mm (3/8 of an inch) in diameter, using a greatly enlarged, triangular labrum as a kind of rolling pin. The female then uses her mandibles to brace the ball of resin against the labrum and flies back to the nest. She lines her brood cell with the resin as a protection from the termites. She then applies a second layer of resin mixed with wood dust and fibers. This dries to form a waterproof layer.

Messer also found that some nests were communal, with several females sharing a common nest entrance.

Resin is also used by many other mason bees. A North American bee, *Anthidiellum notatum*, builds resin cells attached to plant stems.

The majority of mason bees are cavity nesters. The North American Blue Orchard bee (*Osmia lignaria*) favors both beetle borings in dead wood and reed stems while its close Eurasian relative, (see Plate 10-8) the Red Mason bee (*Osmia rufa*) is an opportunist and uses many situations, ranging from beetle borings, nail holes in old mortar and locks. Both species are active in spring and usually build a linear series of cells in a tubular cavity, each cell separated from its neighbor by a wall of mud, with completed nests sealed with a plug of mud.

This opportunism makes them ideal candidates for occupying artificial nests and management as orchard pollinators. (see Plate 10-9)

Carder bees

Females of these bees, *Anthidium* spp. and some related genera, gather the dense velvety down of certain plants to line and seal cells and nests. They use their jaws to tease together or "card" (to use a term from the textile industry) a ball of cotton wool, with which they line and seal cells and nests. (Plate 3-11).

The widespread Eurasian Wool Carder bee (*Anthidium manicatum*) was accidentally introduced into both New Zealand and the Eastern United States and has become well-established in some areas. Human commerce in the form of the timber trade is the most likely mode of accidental introduction of megachilid bees which nest in beetle borings. *Anthidium maculosum* is a close North American relative of *A. manicatum*.

Species of African carder bees (*Serapista* spp.) use plant hairs mixed with animal hairs to create a kind of felt with which they build exposed nests on plants stems.

Plate 3-10. A female mason bee, *Megachile (Chalicodoma) siculum* lays an egg on her completed pollen store. She makes a cluster of such cells and then covers this with a layer of mud. Jordan Valley, Israel. Credit: Ken Preston-Mafham/PremaPhotos Wildlife.

Carpenter bees

These bees make their nests by excavating burrows in solid plant material. The dwarf carpenter bees (*Ceratina* spp.) and the related genus, *Pithitis*, nest in broken pithy stems such as those of bramble, elder or sunflowers.

Unlike the mason bees, females of *Ceratina* spp. do not collect building materials with which to partition and seal cells and close nests. They use pith from within their nesting stem for this purpose.

The giant carpenter bees, *Xylocopa* spp., nest in solid wood. The genus includes some of the largest and most robust of all bees (Plates 2-4, 4-3) and most species occur in the tropics. They use wood fibers stripped from the sides of their nest burrows to construct cell partitions.

Females lay relatively few eggs, as little as four in some species, and the eggs are very large. This probably relates to the large amounts of time and energy involved in burrowing into solid timber. Nest construction is slow and females are often sufficiently long-lived—twelve months or more—to be alive when their offspring become adult. In such cases, the females remain as guards against predatory and parasitic insects. They also protect against other nest-seeking females, which sometimes try to take over nests for their own use. Such females clear out the brood and stored pollen from nests they usurp.

Some species of both dwarf and giant carpenter bees are primitively social. (see Chapter 4).

Plate 3-11. A female European Wool Carder bee, *Anthidium manicatum*, collecting plant hairs to construct its brood cells. Credit: Andreas Müller.

Plate 3–11

Solitary Bees

Plate 4-1

Social Bees

4

The simplest form of sociality in bees involves a certain level of tolerance between a group nesting females. Such a group is said to be **communal**: two or more females share a common nest entrance and main tunnels, but each has her own side branches and cells. This can be likened to an apartment block, where each resident has his or her own apartment, but where there are shared areas such as the entrance, lobbies, and landings.

The widespread Eurasian mining bee, *Andrena carantonica*, is one such species. (see Plate 4-1) Working in Sweden, the British bee scientist, Robert Paxton and colleagues found up to 594 bees living communally (reported in two papers under the names *A. jacobi* and *A. scotica*) and showed that as many as 70% of females mate in the nest with nestmate males. In England I have found communal nests of this species with 9–16 females, though in midland Britain, the species is often solitary.

The North American Trout Lily Sand bee, *A. erythronii*, is also sometimes communal, as is the South American metallic green sweat bee, *Augochloropsis diversipennis*. Such species, for which this lifestyle is not a fixed feature, are said to be **facultatively communal**.

Plate 4-1. A female andrenid mining bee, *Andrena carantonica*. Females of this bee live in communal nests, but also sometimes live as solitary bees. Credit: Henk Wallays. (see page 68)

Plate 4-2. A male orchid bee, *Euglossa imperialis*, a species which ranges from Mexico to the Amazon Basin. Females of this species are possibly quasisocial and, like the males, are bright metallic green. What might appear to be a sting protruding from the end of its abdomen is in fact the end of its tongue, hence the generic name *Euglossa*. Male orchid bees gather scents from orchids and other sources store them in their expanded hind tibiae. (see Chapter 8). Credit: Bernhard Jacobi.

Bees: A Natural History

Plate.4-2

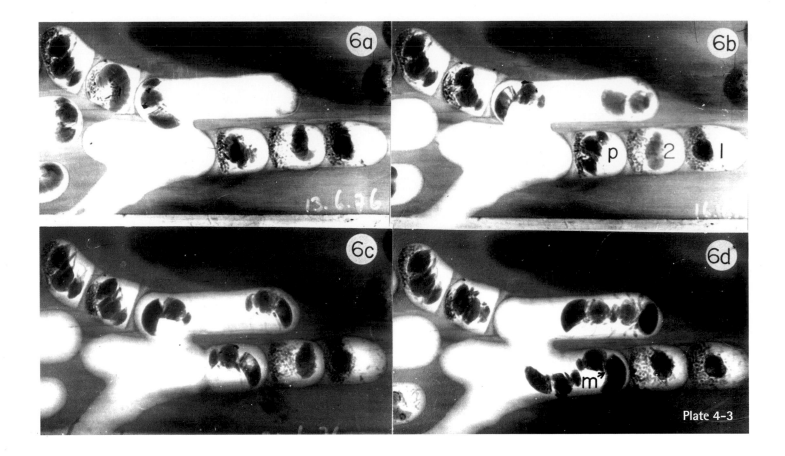

Plate 4-3

The factors which trigger communality in a given population are not understood. It may be something as mundane as the availability of a soil surface that is easily worked. It has been suggested that the coming and going of bees in and out of a busy communal nest might give some protection against cuckoo bees. I have found, however, communally nesting populations of *Andrena carantonica* in which two cuckoo bee species, *Nomada flava* and *N. marshamella*, entered nests frequently. It is worth noting that female *Andrena* do not have a functional sting.

For some species of *Andrena*, the communal nesting habit is a fixed feature. Two Eurasian bees, *A. ferox* and *A. bucephala*, are examples. These species are said to be obligatley communal. In one Oxfordshire locality, I found females of *A. carantonica* sharing a communal nest with *A. bucephala*.

One neighboring nest of the latter proved to have 200+ sharing females and the traffic in and out of the nest was not sufficient to deter its host-specific cuckoo, *Nomada bucephalae*.

There are many more examples of communal bees among species and genera which are predominantly solitary. They still share two main features of strictly solitary species: each cell is mass-provisioned; there is no co-operation between females and no overlap of generations. It is unlikely that communal species gave rise to any evolutionary lines which led to highly social behavior.

In addition to communality there are levels of social behavior in which there is some co-operation between females. **Quasisocial** colonies comprise a group of females of the same generation, all of which have functioning ovaries, are mated and forage for pollen and nectar. There are no structural differences between nestmates, but they have taken the social contract beyond mutual tolerance: at any given time, there are fewer completed, sealed cells than females, indicating that cells are lined, and provisioned by more than one female.

There is, however, only ever one egg laid per cell. This means that although an individual female may contribute to the construction and provisioning of a given cell, she does not necessarily get to lay one of her eggs in it. Nevertheless, in this situation, she can be sure that when she does lay an egg in a cell, she did not necessarily do all the work towards it; the pay-off for the individual thus resides in delayed, reciprocal altruism.

Quasisocial colonies are relatively rare and may be temporary stages in the development of higher levels of sociality. The apid mining bee genus, *Exomalopsis*, is one of the best examples. These New World bees are mainly tropical but several species live in the United States. In Jamaica, Anthony Raw found up to 19 females living in quasisocial colonies. Some Indian halictids, *Nomia* spp., are thought to live in similar colonies and in Costa Rica, R. B. Roberts found a colony of the large, brilliant metallic orchid bee, *Euglossa imperialis* with all the apparent hallmarks of quasisociality: fewer open, incomplete cells than the associated eight females. Female *Euglossa*, however, often return to their natal nests shortly after emergence, so the quasisocial status of this species is not yet established with certainty. (Plate 4-2)

Semisocial colonies also comprise an association of females of the same generation. But there is a major difference here: although the bees are outwardly similar, dissection shows that a proportion of the bees have undersized ovaries and rarely lays eggs; these are often unmated and are mainly cell-constructors and foragers. Others, with enlarged, active ovaries, are the principal egg-layers. This is a form of division of a labor, a primitive hint of the situation in the highly social stingless honeybees and true honeybees.

Semisocial colonies are particularly numerous among the very many North and South American species of sweat bee (Halictidae). Even species which are normally communal may sometimes have semisocial colonies. This suggests that at these grades of sociality, the situation at the level of the local population may be fluid. The semisocial habit, however, is a fixed feature of some species such as the Amazon metallic sweat bee *Augochloropsis sparsilis* and other sweat bees in the genus *Pseudaugochloropsis*.

Subsocial colonies differ from all of the above types of sociality in that they comprise a family group, with one adult female and her offspring. Unlike the solitary bees, where the female seals her egg in a cell with all the food needed for development (mass provisioning), the female feeds her offspring during the course of their development. This is termed progressive feeding. Subsocial nests are found most frequently in the twelve genera of the tribe Allodapini (Apidae). These are dwarf carpenter bees which excavate their nests in pithy stems.

In some bees the subsocial life-style is a stage in the development of more complex colonies. For example, all bumblebee colonies are initially subsocial while the immature offspring are cared for by the foundress queen.

One species of giant carpenter bee, *Xylocopa pubescens* has an unusual variation on the subsocial lifestyle. This species is found in Africa and the Middle East and has been well studied in Israel by Dan Gerling and his colleagues, using X-ray techniques to record activities within the nests (Plate 4-3); Katja Hogendoorn and colleagues have also made important contributions to our knowledge of this bee.

The females bore into solid wood to make nest tunnels, starting in February-March. They behave as solitary bees until the first generation offspring emerge in May and June. Unusually, the newly emerged adults remain teneral, that is, their wings are not fully hardened. One or two teneral females take up guard duties at the nest entrance when their mother is away

---

Plate 4–3. X-ray photographs of a nest of the carpenter bee, *Xylocopa pubescens*, taken at different stages of it development in Israel. The nest was excavated in solid wood. 6a. shows the nest foundress and four cells containing immatures.
6c. shows foundress and two newly-emerged females. 6d. shows liquid food exchange or trophallaxis between the mother bee, "m" and one of her daughters.
Credit: Dan Gerling.

Plate 4–4

Plate 4–4. Laden with pollen, a female sweat bee, *Lasioglossum malachurum*, retruns to her nest. The guard bees of this primitively eusocial Eurasian bee will let her in when they have established her credentials by scent. Credit: Andrej Gogala.

on foraging trips. She provides pollen, stored in a slanted heap in a branch of the tunnel, on which her daughters feed. She also feeds them directly, tongue-to-tongue, with nectar. This is a process called **trophallaxis** and is a feature of the more complex colonies of bumblebees, stingless bees and honeybees.

When their wings are fully hardened, some of the offspring females leave to mate and found their own nests. Some remain and add their own nest tunnels to the branched system, co-existing with their long-lived mother as they store pollen and lay eggs. The females take turns in jointly guarding the nest. There may be three or four generations throughout the season, which ends in October. Adult males and females overwinter in nest burrows and the cycle begins anew the following February.

Often, there is competition for access to nest sites, especially in extreme desert conditions and established nests of Indian carpenter bees are often usurped by other females.

The most complex of insect societies are said to be **eusocial**. These include the termites (Order: Isoptera) and ants, the social wasps such as hornets and yellow-jackets, many species of sweat bees, the bumblebees, stingless honeybees and the true honeybees. In eusocial colonies there are two or more generations and a distinct division of labor. There is usually a single egg layer, the queen (often called a **gyne**), and a caste of more or less sterile females, the workers.

The simplest of these are the mining bees, usually referred to in North America as sweat bees and they are often referred to as primitively eusocial. With these bees there are no distinct structural differences between the queen and workers, though the queen is usually larger.

The most iconic of **primitively eusocial** sweat bees is the North American *Lasioglossum zephyrum*, which was studied for many years by Charles Michener and his colleagues and students of the University of Kansas at Lawrence.

As with all social sweat bees, each nest is founded in spring by a lone female. She excavates a nest tunnel in the ground and, as with almost all solitary mining bees, lines the cells with the Dufour's gland secretion (see Chapter 3). Here the resemblance ends: the females of all sweat bees, solitary or social, hibernate in their old nests after mating in the late summer or early autumn of the previous year. This eliminates the need to mate before founding her nest.

Colonies of *L. zephyrum* are annual and have 4-45 females. A founding female constructs three or four cells and in each stores a ball of pollen moistened with nectar on which she lays a single egg. She thus behaves like a typical solitary bee. Her adult daughters emerge and remain with their natal nest, extending it and constructing cells.

The colony is now at a subsocial stage, but soon, the queen starts to exert dominance over her daughters: she nudges them frequently with her head and this aggression inhibits the development of their ovaries. At the same time, they start to provision the cells: they have become workers and the colony is now eusocial.

Apart from laying eggs on the pollen balls of completed cells, the female spends time inspecting cells. She also spends some time directing the behavior of workers: she waits just inside the nest entrance or at branches in the nest tunnel, places where she is likely to meet returning pollen-laden workers. She backs away, drawing a worker to cells that need pollen.

Unlike many sweat bees, the first generation of offspring includes males and some workers mate and lay eggs. Those with the largest ovaries tend to act as guard bees.

The founding queen dies in June and those daughters and granddaughters which have mated start to lay eggs. The colony reverts to a quasisocial or semisocial state. The remaining mated females hibernate in the nest until the following spring.

Lasioglossum is one of the largest genera of sweat bees. Some are solitary but the genus includes almost all types of social behavior. In Eurasia, two eusocial species have been well-studied: Mediterranean populations of *L. malachurum* (Plate 4-4) have larger colonies than those in Britain and differ in that brood cells remain open during larval development and males are produced only after the production of two or three female generations. *L. marginatum* is unusual in that the queens live for up to five or six years.

Bumblebees

A fully-developed colony of bumblebees (*Bombus* spp.) (see Plates 2-4 and 4-5) is eusocial, but each starts as a subsocial unit comprising a queen and her immediate offspring. In temperatte regions, queen bumblebees emerge from hibernation and search for suitable nest sites. Each mated the previous summer and spent the winter dormant in a small cell excavated in the soil a few centimeters deep. She lives off body fat accumulated by intensive feeding in the weeks before entering dormancy.

Dependent on species, nest sites can be above ground in dense grass tussocks or in old mouse burrows. The Eurasian Tree bumblebee, *Bombus hypnorum*, uses old bird nests in trees. This species was first recorded in the United Kingdom in 2001 and in twelve years has rapidly spread northwards several hundred miles (See Chapter 14).

Having chosen a suitable nest, the queen secretes wax from abdominal glands and uses this, mixed with pollen, to build a single cell. Here, she deposits pollen and within this lays about a dozen eggs; adjacent to this cell, she builds a pot in which she stores honey. This is more dilute than that made by honeybees, but is made in much the same way, namely absorbing water from nectar in her honey stomach.

In between foraging trips for more pollen and nectar, the queen lies on top of her brood cell, incubating the eggs using heat generated by high frequency, vibration of flight muscles and also by chemical means. During periods of incubation, the

Plate 4–5. Inside the nest of a North American bumblebee, *Bombus occidentalis*. Workers tend their developing sisters, one of which has just returned with a full pollen load. This species is a pollen-storer rather than a pocket maker. Berkeley, California. (see Plate 13-2) Credit: Edward Ross.

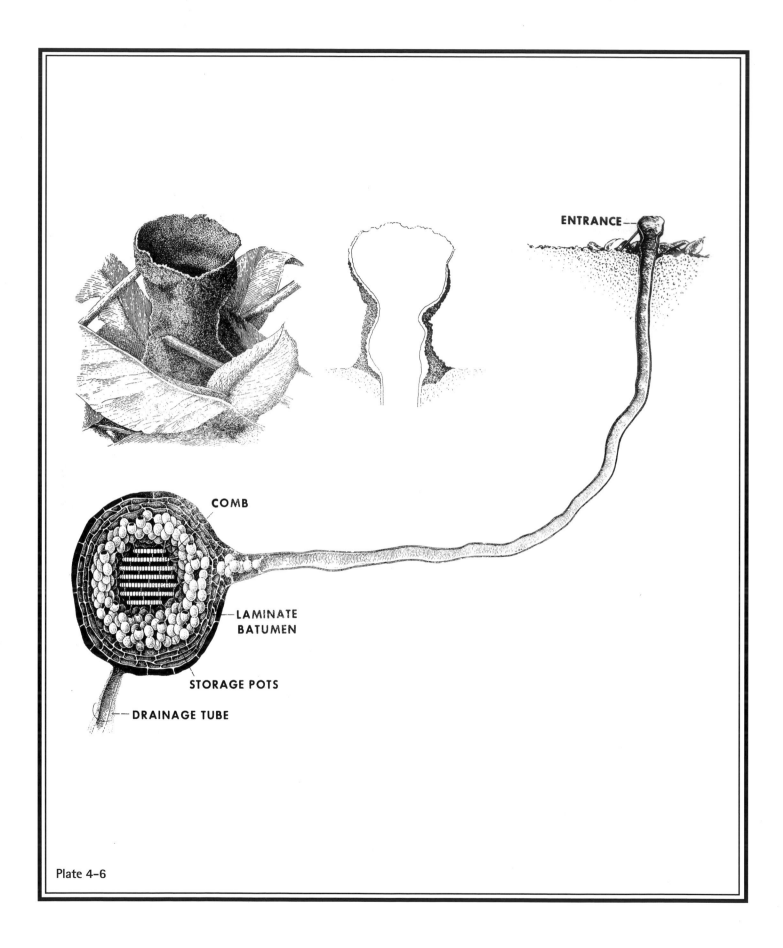

ENTRANCE

COMB

LAMINATE
BATUMEN

STORAGE POTS

DRAINAGE TUBE

Plate 4–6

queen maintains an internal body temperature of 37–39°C (98.6–102.2°F), enabling her to keep her brood at 30–32°C (86–89.6°F). If the weather is unsuitable for foraging, she feeds on her honey store, which is within reach, so that she doesn't have to leave the brood cell.

Within four days the eggs hatch and the larvae eat the pollen. Initially, they live within a cavity in the pollen mass, the brood clump. Eventually, the queen surrounds each larva with its own wax cell and she enlarges this as the larva grows.

Bumblebee larvae are fed in one of two ways, according to species. In some, termed pollen-storers, the original brood clump separates and the larvae construct their own individual cells from wax pieces which they bind together with silk. (Plate 4-5) The queen feeds them individually with regurgitated nectar and pollen.

The species of bumblebee which practice the other mode of larval feeding are called pocket makers: here, the queen adds pockets of pollen to the brood clump and the larvae continue their collective feeding. Later in their development, the queen makes holes in the wax covering of the clump and, like the pollen-storers, begins progressive feeding, regurgitating a nectar and pollen mixture onto the larvae.

The larvae have four stages, each separated by a molt of their soft cuticle. After 10–14 days they spin a tough silk cocoon and pupate. The queen and, later, workers, remove the wax forming the brood cells and use it elsewhere.

The pupal stage lasts 2 weeks, so the total development time from egg to adult is 4 to 5 weeks.

Occasionally, some of the first brood of workers may be too small to fly. In this case, the queen continues to forage and the workers confine themselves to tasks in the nest repairing cells, re-cycling wax, etc. As new generations of larger workers come on stream, the queen assumes what will be her major role for the rest of the colony cycle: egg-laying. By now, the workers will have taken over all foraging, with younger individuals initially concentrating on nest maintenance and assisting the queen with brood care.

Some larger workers may lay eggs which the usually queen usually destroys if she finds them. Because workers are unmated, any eggs which escape the queen's attention will produce only males. As the colony increases in size, it is more difficult for the queen to destroy worker eggs and these make an increasing contribution to male production and may well account for most of the males produced by a colony. Towards the end of the cycle, the foundress queen produces both males and new queens. The males leave the nest and feed at flowers and seek mates (see Chapter 5). After mating, the new generation of queens seek suitable places in which to spend their dormant period until the following spring.

The ultimate size of a bumblebee colony never rivals that of stingless honeybees and true honeybees. The largest recorded colony was found in Mexico, in the North American species *Bombus medius*, containing 2,184 workers.

Plate 4-6. Top left: The nest entrance turret of the South American stingless bee, *Trigona recursa*. Middle: section through the turret showing the expanded space in which guard bees wait. Right: Entrance turret protruding through leaf litter on forest floor. Center, section through whole nest. The central horizontal comb contains the developing brood, and the bullet-shaped cells are storage pots for pollen and honey. The nest is protected by an outer layer, batumen, a resistant mixture of wax, resin, mud and, sometimes, animal feces and which also forms the lining of the nest tunnel and the body of the entrance turret. The drainage tube is an essential structure for ground-nesting species in tropical rain forest. Credit: J. M. F. Camargo, 1970, *Revista Biologia Tropical* 16 : 207–39/C. D. Michener/Harvard University Press.

Plate 4-7

Bees: A Natural History

Stingless bees (Apidae: Meliponini) comprise at least 300 species found in both the Old and New World tropics, with the greatest diversity of genera and species in Central and South America.

The oldest known bee is a fossil stingless bee, *Cretotrigona prisca*, found in amber in New Jersey. It is structurally very similar to modern stingless bees (*Trigona* spp.). The fact that the oldest known bee species is a member of a highly eusocial group is intriguing. It means that social behavior in bees is ancient, dating from at least 96–74 million years ago.

The Mayan Stingless bee (*Melipona beecheii*) is managed by the indigenous peoples of Central America and was almost certainly the source of honey presented to Columbus and his crew when they set foot in the New World. This is one of the largest of stingless bees, similar in size to the Western honeybee (*Apis mellifera*) and is managed for honey production in traditional hollow log or clay hives.

Although highly social, with distinct division of labor, stingless bees differ from bumblebees and honeybees in one important way: they resemble solitary bees in practicing mass provisioning rather than progressive feeding, eggs being laid by queens in provisioned cells, which workers then seal.

Stingless bees nest in pre-existing cavities such as holes in the ground and hollow logs or sometimes in the sides of termite nests. For nest-building materials, they secrete wax and mix it with resin and gums collected at plant wounds, often mixed with animal faeces or mud. There is a wide range of architectural types (Plate 4-6). Many species build characteristic turrets as part of their nest entrances (Plate, 4-7).

The tasks performed by the workers of stingless bees are age-related: for the first few weeks a worker is a house bee, receiving food from returning foragers and secreting wax for cell construction. She becomes a

Plate 4-7. Stingless bees, *Trigona* sp., at nest entrance on tree trunk. Rainforest, La Selva Biological Station, Costa Rica. Credit: Adrian Hepworth.

Plate 4-9

Bees: A Natural History

these natural situations or in the hives provided by beekeepers, comb-building workers perform this intricate work using their manibles to shape the wax. That they can do this in complete darkness is a tribute to their tactile and maniulatives skills.

As well as wax, honeybees use plant resins, sometimes mixed with wax, to seal gaps in the hive or nest. This sweet-smelling substance is called propolis.

The house bees also keep the colony clean, removing dead larvae and adults. They also feed the queen and place honey and pollen in storage cells. Towards the end of her period as a house bee, the worker acts as a guard at the hive or nest entrance and sometimes takes part in communal fanning behavior, using her wings to direct cool air into the hive in periods of hot weather.

Guards will attack and sting any intruder into the hive, whether a mouse, or bees from other colonies. Guards recruit other workers to assist in defense by emitting an alarm pheromone from a gland at the base of the sting apparatus.

More often than not, stinging results in the death of the worker: the sting is armed with backwardly-directed spines, which engage with the tissues of the victim. When a worker struggles to release herself, the sting and its associated venom glands remains behind, with the muscles of the venom gland still visibly pumping venom. (Plate 13-1)

A worker, which has survived her period of guarding behavior now joins the cohort of field bees, whose main task is to gather pollen and nectar for conversion into honey. Her first task as a field bee is to memorize both near and far landmarks for orientation back to the nest, as outlined in Chapter 1. She will forage regularly between 6 and 9km (3.7–5.6 miles) from the colony.

Plate 4-9 Two workers of the Western Honeybee, *Apis mellifera*, on honey storage comb. One is a returned field bee which is handing over nectar to a house bee by tongue-to-tongue contact, a process called trophallaxis. Mature honey is clearly visible in the hexagonal cells. Credit: Edward Ross.

membership of workers attending the queen and thus queen substance is transmitted throughout the colony. It requires a daily dose of only one millionth of a gram of queen substance to maintain suppression of the workers' ovaries.

As with stingless bees, swarming is the means of colony reproduction. In temperate regions, this usually takes place in late spring or early summer, when stored honey is plentiful in the colony. The death of the queen honeybee is one stimulus for workers to prepare for a swarm. Experiments have shown that if a queen is removed from a colony, workers actively search for her within 15-30 minutes. They change the feeding pattern of a few larvae to an exclusive diet of royal jelly in order to raise new queens. Because queens are larger than workers, they increase the size of the cells involved.

The other stimulus for a swarm is the failing powers of an aging queen: she begins to lay far fewer than the normal 2000 eggs per day and/or produces less queen substance. There may also be a dilution effect if the colony has become so large that workers are no longer receiving their full daily dose of queen substance. In these situations, the workers also rear new queens in preparation for swarm.

Queens take about two weeks to develop and during this time, the workers are aggressive towards the old queen, biting and pulling at her legs.

The first of the new queens to emerge seeks out and breaks into the other queen cells and then stings them to death. She then leaves on a mating flight and afterwards returns to the colony.

Meanwhile, it is the old queen who ultimately leaves with the swarm. Prior to this, the workers fill

---

Plate 4–11. A queen *Apis mellifera*, marked with red paint for ease of recognition, is attended by her court of workers. Their constant antennation of her body monitors her reproductive state. They also lick her, absorbing "queen substance" which exerts control over their ovaries, keeping them sterile. Credit: Edward Ross.

Plate 4-11

Bees: A Natural History

Plate 4–12

their honey-crops with honey and scouts will have found a suitable place where the swarm assembles, often in the branches of a tree, a fence or the sides of a building. (see Plate 4-12)

Once the swarm is assembled, scout bees again go searching, this time for a permanent site for the colony. Scout bees return to the hanging swarm and communicate and run about over their nestmates, using the dance language to communicate the distance and direction of the new nest site.

The swarm gradually re-locates and workers start secreting wax and constructing new comb.

Why be social?

With the exception of termites, it is the Hymenoptera—ants, wasps and bees—which, time and again, have evolved eusociality. With hymenopterans this can involve not only self-sacrificing colony defense behavior, but invariably, a worker caste which does not reproduce, but which labors intensively to rear the offspring of another female, the queen.

How can a non-reproductive caste pass on any genes for altruistic behavior? It seems that there is something about the Hymenoptera which predisposes them to become social in these ways and appear to be altruistic. In fact, social behavior has evolved 12 times in the insects, 11 of them in the Hymenoptera. An Oxford-based ecological geneticist, the late Bill Kemp, ultimately found the answer to the conundrum: what is the pay-off in either sacrificing one's life and/or contributing to the reproductive success of another individual?

The answer lies in the skewed levels of kinship in the Hymenoptera, including the bees. The skew results from the method of sex determination. Under normal circumstances, all males are derived from unfertilized eggs. In other words, they only receive maternal genes and thus only have half the normal complement. They are said to be haploid and all their genes are identical; this method of sex determination is called haplodiploidy. Because females are derived from fertilized eggs, they receive genes from both father and mother and are said to be diploid.

This results in a distortion of the normal degrees of kinship between females: a female shares only 50% of her genes with her daughters, but, on average, 75% with her sisters. A eusocial colony is thus a sorority of females where, if an individual worker does not reproduce, but helps raise an egg to become a reproducing sister (a queen), then her pay-off is that 75% of her genes rather than 50% pass into the next generation. If she sacrifices her life to enhance this sisterly reproduction by proxy, then she enjoys the same pay-off.

This is the so-called theory of "kin selection" and it takes the altruism out of altruism.

Can honeybees inform the search for extra-terrestrial intelligent life?

Science fiction movies and books often depict extra-terrestrial intelligent beings as bipedal humanoids with large heads and almond-shaped eyes.

Academics involved in the search for extra-terrestrial intelligence (SETI) also often postulate the bi-pedal humanoid form such beings would take. They also cite the development of symbolic language as a prerequisite for the definition of intelligent life.

Honeybees have evolved a basic symbolic language that includes not only the informative dance language but use it in combination with high frequency buzzes as part of their system of communication.

This, together with their complex systems of pheromonal communication, both within the nest and at flowers (Chapter 6) and their ability to manipulate wax in highly precise ways, suggests strongly that we need not necessarily expect any intelligent extra-terrestrial beings to resemble ourselves in appearance or structure.

This would be likely in planets with a longer history of life and with different early evolutionary events than ours.

Plate 4-12. A honeybee swarm temporarily clustered on a chestnut tree. Leicestershire, England. Credit: Christopher O'Toole.

Plate 5-1

The Male of the Species

5

Bees are in business to make more bees. Females do this via considerable investments of time and energy in searching for nest sites, constructing nests and foraging for nectar and pollen.

Males do not have to multi-task to such an extent. They invest their entire time and energy budget in seeking to mate with as many females as possible. This is not true, however, of the males of the 11 species of *Apis*, the true honeybees: they invest their entire lives in a single, fatal mating.

The males of a few species, however, are exceptional in other ways—apart from mate-seeking, the males of four species of North American bumblebee (*Bombus* spp.) also incubate brood rather like workers (see Chapter 4). The males of some South American *Melipona* and *Trigona* spp. secrete wax and use it to build honey storage pots and brood cells. They also carry out another duty usually reserved for workers: they receive nectar from incoming workers and place it in storage pots. David W. Roubik, a Smithsonian tropical research scientist, has observed male *Melipona marginata* actually involved in the ripening of nectar to convert it into honey.

The females in the majority of solitary and primitively social species mate only once; they store sperm in a special sac, the **spermatheca**. This contains enough sperm for their entire reproductive needs.

Plate 5-1. A North American mining bee, *Anthophora bomboides*, visits a Cobweb thistle, *Cirsium occidentale*. Credit: Edward Ross. (see page 92)

Plate 5-2. Long-horned mining bees, *Eucera* sp., sleeping in a Buttercup, *Ranunculus* sp., Oukaïmeden, Morocco. Male solitary bees often sleep communally in flowers. This habit contributes some pollination services: the jostling for position and moving on to find other floral roosts of the same species contributes to pollen transfer. Credit: Edward Ross.

Bees: A Natural History

Plate 5-2

Plate 5–5

noted similar behavior in the Negev desert by males of *Xylocopa pubescens*.

The most frequent type of territory, though, is centered on a patch of flowers providing forage for females. Male behavior in the European Wool Carder bee, *Anthidium manicatum*, is a good example of resource-based territoriality. This species was accidentally introduced into North America and New Zealand and is now established in both areas. The native North American Wool Carder bee (*A. maculosum*) has very similar behavior.

The species is unusual in two ways: almost all males are larger than the females and the females mate more than once. Males establish territories at clumps of plants, such as Lamb's Ears (*Stachys byzantinum* and *St. sylvatica*), sages (*Salvia* spp.) or Horehound (*Marrubium vulgare*). These plants are not only sources of nectar and pollen for foraging females, for some, such as the species of *Stachys*, also have another resource vital to females: the dense, cottony down that covers their leaves and which the female gather for nest-building purposes (see Chapter 3).

Male *Anthidium manicatum* and their relatives have a rapid, darting flight, combined with the ability to decelerate rapidly, hover and fly backwards. These flight skills are adaptations to the aggressive defense of their territories, which they patrol for hours, resting occasionally to refuel on nectar.

They dart at rival males and other bees, which they attack and sometimes injure or even kill. Their arms for such violence are five spines at the tip of the abdomen (Plate 5-5), with which they lunge at intruders, using their flexible abdomens to bring the spines down and forward and crush the insect grasped

Plate 5-5. Abdominal spines of the European Wool Carder bee, *Anthidium manicatum*. These aggressively territorial males use the spines as weapons when attacking rival males and foraging females of other species. Credit: Victor Gonzalez.

Plate 6-1

The Pollination Market

6

Plate 6-2

Flowers are the sex organs of plants and, as in all sexually reproducing species, the sexes have to come together for mating. Being rooted to the spot, they need some outside help to accomplish this. **Pollination** is the process by which various agencies bring this about. It involves the transfer of pollen grains, the male spores, from the anthers of the flower to the surface of the stigma, the visible part of the female reproductive organs. (Plate 6-1)

Sufferers from hay fever know all too well that wind is one of several agencies that move pollen. Grasses (including maize and rice), oaks, hickory, hazel, birches and alders are some of the culprits here; pollination by wind is termed **anemophily**; and plants that rely on wind are said to be **anemophilous**. Wind pollinated plants produce small, dry pollen grains, which are easily borne on the wind. They have no nectaries and have no need for showy petals to attract insects. Instead, their flowers are small, inconspicuous and often presented as pendulous catkins. This does not preclude visitation by bees, however. Some species of solitary bee genera such as *Andrena* and *Osmia*, often gather pollen from oak catkins and bees sometimes harvest pollen from grasses.

Other agencies or **pollinators** are birds, bats, mice and even water. Insects are by far the most important pollinators, including butterflies, flies and beetles. Pollination by insects is termed **entomophily**. Bees, though, are the most efficient facilitators of mating by proxy in the sex lives of plants; this efficiency lies in the very essence of bee-ness: the active collection and manipulation of pollen. A bee scrabbling about a flower, probing for nectar and/or gathering pollen, dislodges pollen from its body onto the receptive stigma of the flower.

About 80 percent of insect pollinated plants are hermaphrodite, with both male and female parts being present in the same flower.

For most plants, only pollen grains from a different individual of the same species will germinate and ultimately fertilize the flower. This is an adaptation to avoid inbreeding, an incest taboo mediated by an incompatibility system built into the chemistry of the stigmatic surface; pollen from the same plant will simply not germinate to produce the pollen tube. This would normally conduct the sperm nucleus from the pollen grain on to the ovary and effect fertilization.

This system depends on bees bringing pollen from other individuals of the same species, a process called **cross-pollination**. The pollination services provided by bees enable flowering plants to reproduce through their female line, by being fertilized with pollen brought by bees from other conspecific individuals and through the male line, via pollen transported to other individual plants.

Cross-pollination maintains genetic diversity. This is the medium through which natural selection favors beneficial traits and ultimately weeds out traits that are deleterious or sub-optimal. And herein lies the role of bees in maintaining this genetic diversity, which has contributed to the species diversity of modern flowering plants over the past 65 million years.

In some plants, if no pollinators have visited a flower and deposited pollen, the stigma eventually becomes receptive to its own pollen and fertilization occurs. In such cases, however, seed production is usually lower than normal.

Plate 6-1. Flower reproductive organs. The brown anthers of this tulip (*Tulipa* sp.) surround the pale stigma. Apart from worker bumblebees and honeybees, tulips are pollinated by male bees which spend the night in the flowers as convenient shelters. Credit: Ingo Arndt. (see page 104)

Plate 6-2. Buzz pollination: using high frequency vibrations of her wing muscles, this female sweat bee, *Augochloropsis metallica*, dislodges pollen from within the anthers of a Buffalo Nightshade flower, *Solanum rostratum*. Arizona. Credit: Mark Moffett / Minden Pictures.

Plate 6-3

Plate 6-3. A radially symmetrical flower, Gum Rock Rose, *Cistus ladanifer*. The dark patches at the base of the petals are nectar guides, which lead foraging bees to the nectary at the base of each petal. Native to the Western Mediterranean, this shrub and several cultivars is widely grown in gardens all over the world. Credit: Christopher O'Toole.

Very many plant species have developed a feature that increases the chances that pollen adheres to a bee's body. This is a sticky layer on the surface of each grain, the so-called pollenkitt. Evergreen shrubs in the genus *Mahonia* have an additional, active way of delivering pollen on to a bee's body. The anther-bearing stamens are highly sensitive to touch and when a bee probes a flower for nectar, they close inward, depositing pollen on the head of the bee. One can easily test this response with flowers of the Oregon Grape (*Mahonia aquifolium*), a North American shrub now widely grown worldwide in temperate climates—simply poke a needle or toothpick into the flowers and watch the anthers bend inwards.

An additional quirk of nature enhances the ability of bees to gather pollen: a bee in flight builds up a positive electric charge on its body surface. This is fortunate because for some reason, the anthers and pollen grains normally have a negative charge, which means that pollen grains are attracted directly to the bee. Electrostatic forces therefore complement the bee's own pollen-gathering behavior; the mechanism is most efficient in fine, dry weather.

Electrostatics is likely to play a particularly important role in a process called **buzz pollination** or **sonication**. This is a feature of plants that shed pollen inside hollow anthers. About 8 percent of the 230,000-plus flowering plant species do this. There is a single pore at the end or on the side of the anther through which pollen exits. Bees have evolved a way of harvesting pollen from such plants. They sit on the flowers and use their indirect flight muscles to generate audible vibrations with a frequency of 50–2000Hz. This dislodges pollen in clouds on to the bee's body. (Plate 6-2) It has been estimated that sonicating bees can generate forces up to 30G. This is close to the record for human tolerance on a rocket sled.

Plants with these features usually have pendulous flowers and the electrostatic charge on visiting bees means that pollen falls down on to the a bee as it buzzes and most of what might be lost to gravity lands directly on to its body. Electrostatic forces can therefore complement the G force generated by bees.

Buzz pollination is important in several crops, especially tomatoes, eggplants and in the production of potato seeds. In Britain and much of Western Europe, captive colonies of Buff-tailed bumblebees (*Bombus terrestris*) pollinate tomatoes grown in glasshouses, the growers harnessing the bees' ability to sonicate. Growers in North and South America use a related species, the Common bumblebee (*B. impatiens*).

A wide range of bees is capable of effecting pollination in this way but, strangely, buzz pollination is not in the behavioral repertoire of honeybees, though they seem able to use their front legs to vibrate pollen out of the poricidal anthers of blueberries.

The shallow, bowl-shaped flowers of many plants, such as buttercups, roses, apples and almonds, are radially symmetrical. That is, it does not matter what radius you bisect the flower along, both halves will be identical. (Plate 6-4) These species have a mass of anther-bearing stamens surrounding the central stigma and a nectary at the base of each petal. It is easy for visiting bees to probe such flowers for nectar and to scrabble for pollen and favors smaller, short-tongued bees, but does not necessarily exclude bees with longer tongues.

Many families of flowering plants, though, have independently evolved a different floral symmetry; this favors large, long-tongued bees, and requires some physical strength. These are the bilaterally symmetrical or **zygomorphic** flowers. Viewed from the front, such flowers seem compressed from side-to-side: there is only one plane of bisection that gives two equal halves. Snapdragons (*Antirrhinum* spp.) are common garden examples and bumblebees are their only effective pollinators. They are large enough and sufficiently strong to pry apart the main upper and lower petals to gain access to nectar and pollen. By filtering out all but the strongest of bees, snapdragons ensure that the vectors of their pollen are members of the large bee guild (see below), which increase the chances that their pollen is transported over longer distances.

The mint family, **Lamiaceae**, contains many of our culinary herbs—sage, rosemary, thyme and oreganum. These, too, have zygomorphic flowers. Sages (*Salvia* spp.) and the deadnettles (*Lamium* spp.) have developed a way of presenting pollen that maximizes the amount used for reproduction, and, at the same, minimizes the amount of pollen that the bees can glean. The strongly curved dorsal petal conceals the long, curved stamens, the anthers and stigma. When a bee lands on the ventral petal and probes the nectary, its weight triggers the stamens to move downwards and brush against the back of the bee, depositing the pollen along a relatively narrow tract.

It is very difficult, if not impossible, for the bee to remove this pollen from a narrow line down its back. When the bee visits another flower, the pollen brushes against the stigma effecting pollination. If the pollen reward for the bee is minimal or zero, this is more than compensated for by the large amounts of nectar produced by such flowers. Here, the plants are juggling the cost-benefit ratio of rewards in favor of lower loss of pollen to bees against a generous amount of nectar.

Flowers of the pea and bean family, Fabaceae, are also zygomorphic. Very many are specialized for the triggered release of pollen. Each flower comprises five petals, a large upper conspicuous one called the **standard** or flag, two side petals or **wings** and a smaller, lower, boat-shaped petal, the **keel**.

The keel encloses the stamens and stigma. There are ten stamens, nine fused at the base to form a tube, into which nectar collects from a central nectary. When a bee lands on the keel, it probes this tube for nectar; its weight depresses the keel, which frees the anther-bearing stamens from below, depositing pollen

Plate 6-4

Plate 6-4. A worker of the Yellow-faced Bumblebee, *Bombus vosnesenskii*, at a flower of broom, *Cytisus* sp. The weight of her body has "tripped" the flower and the bunch of ten stamens has lunged forwards and upwards to deposit pollen on her underside. The bee's pollen basket is full with broom pollen. Paradise Cove, California. Credit: Edward Ross.

Bees: A Natural History

Plate 6-5

on the underside of the bee's abdomen. The release of stamens is sudden and in some species almost explosive. (Plate 6-4)

The detailed mechanics of this process varies with genus. All the pea and bean crops, together with important forage crops such as alfalfa and vetches, have a version of this pollen delivery system. Important landscape shrubs such as gorse and broom are also members of the Fabaceae, as well as the vine *Wisteria* and Judas Tree (*Cercis siliquastrum*).

Because the pollen is deposited on the underside of the bee's abdomen, Leafcutter bees (*Megachile* spp.) are particularly effective pollinators of fabaceous crops. The Alfalfa Leafcutter bee (*M. rotundata*) is the principal managed pollinator of alfalfa in Canada and the United States (see Chapter 10).

The many different relationships between bees and flowering plants are all examples of mutualism, a situation where two or more organisms perform services to the benefit of all concerned. Well-known examples are cleaner fish, which swim in and out of

the jaws of sharks with impunity while eating food remains snagged on the sharks' teeth, and birds called ox-peckers. They walk along the backs of large animals on the African savannahs, feeding on ticks and flies.

The bee-plant mutualism is much more complex and ecologically important than this. Much of the visual impact of a wide range of habitats is the direct result of the pollination services of bees, which play keystone roles in the creation and maintenance of habitats that support a myriad of other species, including our own.

Plate 6–5. A Treasure Flower (*Gazania rigens*) in normal human vision (left) and in simulated bee vision (right). Credit: Klaus Schmitt.

We can consider mutual dependency of bees and flowering plants as a complex market place. This comprises retailers—flowering plants—and consumers, of varying degrees of discrimination—bees. This is an economy based on the unwitting exchange of goods and services by the participants. Plants provide nectar, pollen and, in some cases, oils and scents, the resources needed by bees. In return, bees provide their pollination services.

The situation is a little more complicated than this: retailers and consumers have to make considerable prior investments to buy themselves into this economy. Plants invest time and energy in the chemical synthesis of scents and colored pigments to attract bees into their part of the market. They expend energy in secreting nectar and producing pollen in excess of their own reproductive needs, the surplus being the vital source of protein for the bees' offspring.

Before playing a full part in the market, female bees make considerable prior investments of time and energy in mating, searching for and constructing a nest. While the bees are making these initial investments, they visit flowers for their own immediate energetic needs and will pollinate to a small extent, so some of their nectar gathering here can be regarded as an advance, on account.

Male bees do not collect pollen, but feed on nectar. This will bring about some pollination.

Floral attractants—the dynamics of flower visitation by bees

A flower-rich meadow, prairie or a spring flush in a desert are beautiful to behold. That blaze of color is a riot of floral sexuality, all its members competing to attract the attention of foraging bees.

The particular range of colors is adapted to the color vision of bees. Compared with human color vision, that of bees is shifted towards the blue end of the spectrum. This means that what we see in that flower-rich meadow is rather different to that which bees perceive. (Plate 6-5) Bees would see a yellow treasure flower as mostly black.

Floral color acts as a medium to long distance attractant to foraging bees. Scent is also important; depending on local conditions such as floral diversity, wind speed and direction, it too can be a long distance attractant, though it is more usually guides bees to flowers when they have arrived in the vicinity.

Research has shown that worker honeybees have impressive abilities in discriminating between scents. When presented with 1,816 odor pairs, they were able to distinguish between 1,729 of them. This acute sensitivity enables a honeybee to memorize a scent associated with a rich pollen and/or nectar reward, return repeatedly to a flower-rich patch, and distinguish between the many plant species that might be present.

Such olfactory skills are amazing when one bears in mind that this is in addition to the complex systems of pheromones and other scents workers deal with in the hive, through which they assess the on-going needs of the colony (see Chapter 4). Given the roles of scents in mating behavior and nest recognition, there is every reason to believe that solitary bees may be just as well endowed.

Scent has another role in the bee-plant relationship. Here, the bees rather than flowers produce the scents. Worker bumblebees, some stingless bees and honeybees deposit scent on the petals of flowers they visit. The bees secrete the odors from glands in the feet (tarsi). There is evidence that there are two types of scent—attractants and repellents, the former signaling to colony mates a rich source of nectar and/or pollen, the latter indicating a depleted flower which should be avoided.

Repellent scent marks seem to be effective between members of the same species and different

---

Plate 6-6. A worker honeybee, *Apis mellifera*, clambers between the anther-bearing stamens of a lotus flower, *Nympaea caerulea*. Known also as the Sacred Blue Lily or the Blue Egyptian Lily, this plant appears frequently in ancient Egyptian art, where it is a symbol of the god Nefertem; a tea made from its flowers is said to have sedative properties. Credit: michaeljung © Crestock.

Bees: A Natural History

Plate 6–6

Plate 6-7

Plate 6-7. A female long-horned apid, *Eucera cypria* (Eucerini), deploys her long tongue in readiness for drinking nectar at a vetch blossom, *Vicia* sp. She already has a full pollen load. Yaqum, Israel. Credit: Nicolas J. Vereecken.

colonies and between honeybees and bumblebees. Honeybees and bumblebees are somehow able to match the duration of the repellent scents they deposit to the rate of nectar secretion of given plants. Comfrey flowers (*Symphytum* spp.) replenish nectar rapidly and the repellent scent persists for only a few minutes. Flowers of trefoils and vetches, (*Lotus* spp. and *Melilotus* spp.), replenish nectar slowly and the repellent scent on these plants is effective for 2–24 hrs. It seems, therefore that the bees can modify the volatility of the scents they deposit in balance with their perceived amount of nectar reward. This is yet another example of the decision-making abilities of bees.

The scent marking of flowers is not confined to the highly social bees. Solitary bees in the genera *Colletes*, *Andrena*, *Anthidium*, *Osmia*, *Tetralonia* and *Anthophora* also behave in this way. Not being part of a colony, solitary bees do not use scent to communicate the quality of floral resources to nest mates. Instead, they are *aide-mémoires* for their own individual benefit. In at least one species of *Anthophora*, the deposited scent is a complex blend of volatiles which is individually recognizable and seems to vary with the foraging needs of the bee.

Apart from depositing their own scent marks on flowers, the females of the European Wool Carder bee, *Anthidium manicatum*, avoid flowers scent-marked by Buff-tailed bumblebees, *Bombus terrestris*; furthermore, Buff-tailed workers show a stronger aversion response to scent marks deposited by the carder bee than they do to scents deposited by conspecifics. There may well be a good reason for this. Male carder bees are aggressively territorial at patches of forage plants used by their females, and the

bumblebees may well have learned to associate the scent deposited by female carder bees with a violent attack by male carder bees.

The scent dimension of our flower-rich meadow is undoubtedly more complex than hitherto realized; it is the basis of much current research, all of which points to ultrafine-tuning of bee-plant relationships.

Flowers have one final aid for visiting bees in search of nectar. These are dark pigmented lines or blotches on petals, the **nectar guides**, which direct the bee to the nectaries at the base of the petals. (Plate 6-3)

Some flowers break the bee plant contract by providing bees with only a partial reward or even no reward at all. Poppies (*Papaver* spp.), for example, produce no nectar but do produce copious amounts of pollen. Such plants rely on other plants to provide the nectar that fuels the activities of the bees that pollinate them, and, in so doing, they practice a kind of parasitism.

Within the pollination market, there are two behavioral-ecological guilds—the small bee guild and the large bee guild.

Small Bee Guild: these range in size from 2.0–12mm (0.08-0.5 inches) in length. They are short-tongued bees (0.5–9mm/0.02-0.4in), relatively slow fliers, low energy species associated with shallow, easy access, often radially symmetrical flowers, that offer relatively low nectar rewards. These bees are relatively short distance foragers and include bees in the mining bee families Colletidae, Andrenidae, Halictidae, Melittidae, some of the cavity-nesting Megachilidae and the tribe Exomalopsini of the family Apidae. The stingless honeybees, Meliponini, fall into the category.

Large Bee Guild: these comprise large species (10–50mm/0.4-2in long), fast flying, high-energy bees, which can be long-distance foragers, with long tongues and often associated with tubular, restricted access flowers, with high nectar rewards. This guild includes some Megachilidae, and the Apidae, especially the mining bee tribes Eucerini, Emphorini, Anthophorini, Centridini, Euglossini, Bombini and the Bombini (bumblebees). (Plate 6-8)

Where do the eleven species of honeybee fit in here? The Western honeybee (*Apis mellifera*) is medium sized, as are its Asian relatives, the Asiatic *A. cerana*, Koschevnikov's *A. koschevnikovi*, Sulawesian *A. nigrocincta* and Bornean, *A. nuluensis*. Two other Asian species, the Red Dwarf honeybee, *A. florea*, and Black Dwarf honeybee, *A. andreniformis*, are much smaller. Two honeybee species do fall into the large bee guild, the Giant Honeybee, *A. dorsatal* and its close, high altitude relative, the Giant Himalayan honeybee, *A. laboriosa*, together with the Indonesian *A. binghami* and Philippine honeybee (*A. breviligula*), though the last two may turn out to be regional variants of the Giant Honeybee.

While these generalizations are broadly consistent with bee taxonomy at the family/tribal level, as with all generalizations, there are exceptions. Thus the females of some Mediterranean species of plasterer bees (*Colletes*) are extremely fast flyers, while Western Honeybees though not particularly swift flyers, are long-distance pollinators, regularly foraging up 12km (7.5 miles) from the hive. Other exceptions to the rule are the giant carpenter bees such as *Xylocopa* spp., which include some of the largest and most robust of all bees, but they have relatively short tongues.

Plate 6-8. Long tongues are an adaptation for probing deep-tubed flowers for nectar. Here, though, two females of a species of the apid mining bee genus, *Amegilla*, drink water from damp sand. In hot, dry conditions, this is also a way of replenishing body salt levels. Dundo, Angola. Credit: Edward Ross.

Bees: A Natural History

Plate 6-8

The Pollination Market

Plate 6-9

Bees: A Natural History

siliquastrum) in the Judean Mountains of Israel. The lights from nearby Palestinian villages may have aided them in their activities.

There is, however, one large oriental carpenter bee, *Xylocopa tranquebarica*, which is truly nocturnal. Studies in India and Thailand have shown that this bee can forage on moonless nights, using starlight for navigation. Unusual for bees, it can see colors at these low light intensities. Hawkmoths and geckos were, until recently, the only know exponents of nocturnal color vision.

Xylocopa tranquebarica can fly at temperatures as low as 12°C (53.6°F) and another oriental nocturnal species, *X. tenuiscapa*, forages at 2–14°C (35.6–57.2°F). Endothermy almost certainly enables these large nocturnal bees to warm up to flight temperature.

Almost all crepuscular, nocturnal and matinal bees have enlarged compound eyes and many have larger simple eyes (ocelli—see Chapter 1) than their diurnal relatives. These are modifications to capture as much light as possible at low light intensities.

The sophisticated optical physiology of these bees is only part of an array of behavioral adaptations found generally among bees: the ability to associate the multi-channel signaling systems of flowering plants with the rewards on offer and to discriminate between these rewards based on their immediate energetic needs.

These bee-plant contracts comprise complex, nested chains of relationships that are the sustaining framework for much of life on Earth.

Plate 6–9. A White-tailed bumblebee worker, *Bombus lucorum*, coming in for a landing on an apple blossom with its legs already laden with pollen. Trowbridge, Wiltshire, England. Credit: Lawrence Martin.

Plate 7-1

Squash Bees and Other Pollen Specialists

7

The male and female flowers of squashes and pumpkins are borne on separate plants, so they require insects to effect pollination. Commercial growers of these crops in North America often rent beehives for pollination purposes. This can frequently be an unnecessary expense because, ranging from home gardens to huge monoculture fields, native bees are responsible in very many places for most of the pollination of these native crop plants.

The bees involved are called squash bees; they are solitary mining bees, *Peponapis* (13 spp.) and *Xenoglossa* (7 spp.) in the family Apidae. These bees often nest in dense aggregations and the females restrict their pollen gathering solely to the squash and pumpkin genus *Cucurbita* (Family: Cucurbitaceae). Squash bees are found all over North America and there are tropical representatives in Central and South America. (see Plate 7-1 page 124)

The hairs comprising the scopa on the females' hind legs are coarse, un-branched, and straight: adaptations for the handling and transport of the large pollen grains typical of cucurbits. Although honeybees visit squash flowers for nectar and pollinate a few flowers, their pollen baskets do not cope well with this type of pollen. Because squash bees are active in the early morning, often at dawn, well before honeybees become active, they pollinate almost all available flowers, so later visits by honeybees are often superfluous.

USDA bee scientist Jim Cane and colleagues showed that male squash bees contribute significantly to pollination: they seek mates at squash flowers in very large numbers.

The annual yield of squashes and related crops in the United States is worth half a billion dollars; the squash bees are thus one of the best examples of how unmanaged wild bees which are pollen specialists can be of great economic importance. The bees are widespread and common and account for almost all the pollination of squashes and pumpkins grown in backyards; the domestication of squashes by Native Americans was entirely dependent on native squash bees: it occurred long before European settlers introduced the honeybee to the Americas.

At the moment, there are no active measures to conserve squash bees, but it would be useful if both farmers and backyard growers were aware of their nesting requirements: patches of bare earth in marginal situations. So far, these bees have been very good at looking after themselves because the ranges of some species have expanded to follow the spread of crop plantings.

The fifty or so species of North American sunflowers comprise another group of plants, which are pollinated by a cohort of pollen specialists. All except one require cross-pollination in order to set seed. This is not without economic interest: sunflower oil, from seeds of the commercially grown species, *Helianthus annus*, is one of the top four sources of culinary oils.

Sunflowers (*Helianthus* spp.) are well pollinated by honeybees, but native American bees are also important: 39 species are primary specialists, that is, they specialize almost entirely on the pollen of *Helianthus* species. A further 92 are termed secondary specialists in that they specialize on the pollen of the daisy family of flowering plants, the Asteraceae, to which sunflowers belong. In North America, a total of 284 bee species regularly gather nectar and/or pollen from sunflowers. This figure includes bees which are not pollen specialists.

The fact that some bee species are more narrowly specialist than others has led to a classification of relationships between bees and their pollen sources. Bees which are generalists are said to be **polylectic**. Most bees are polylectic, especially social species: they have to be, because they are active for far longer than the flowering periods of most plants. Bees which collect pollen from

---

Plate 7-1. A female squash bee, *Peponapis pruinosa*, at a sectioned squash flower, *Cucurbita* sp., with cucumber beetles, *Acalymma* undecimpunctata. Credit: Edward Ross. (see page 124)

a restricted range of flowering plants are termed **oligolectic** and their flight period always coincides very closely with the flowering season of the plants on which they specialize.

Bees which specialize on the pollen of a particular flowering plant family are termed **broadly oligolectic**. Examples here are Eurasian plasterer bee, *Colletes daviesanus*, whose females specialize on flowers of the daisy family Asteraceae.

The primary sunflower specialists, which only forage on sunflower pollen, are termed **narrowly oligolectic**. Other examples are the Eurasian Harebell Mason bee, *Chelostoma campanularum*, which restricts its pollen gathering to bellflowers in the genus *Campanula*. Very often, as with the Harebell Carpenter bee, the scientific name of the bee reflects the identity of the pollen host. The same is true of another Eurasian species, the Mallow Longhorn bee (*Tetralonia malvae*), which specializes on the pollen of mallows, *Malva* species, in the plant family Malvaceae. Similarly, the North American Trout Lily Sand bee, (*Andrena erythronii*) is oligolectic on Trout Lily (*Erythronium americanum*).

Bee species whose females use the pollen of only one plant species are termed monolectic. Such bees are relatively rare and the concept of monolecty is not recognized by all bee scientists.

Oligolecty is widespread among solitary bees. The plasterer bees (*Colletes* spp.) have many examples of the different grades of oligolecty. Table 1 summarizes this for six Eurasian species. The members of the *C. succinctus* species group are of particular interest. These species all nest in dense aggregations and are very closely related and difficult for the non-specialist to separate. Indeed, *C. hederae* was only recognized as a distinct species in 1993. Hitherto, it was confused with *C. halophilus*.

In Britain this species is rapidly expanding its range. In the late 1990's it was known from a few localities along the south coast. Now its range extends to Oxford, a northward range expansion of 163km (101 miles), a rate of just over 12km (7.5 miles) per year and westward to sites in South Wales 103km (64 miles), an annual rate of 8km (5 miles).

The Ivy Plasterer bee, *Colletes hederae*, is monolectic on English ivy *Hedera helix* and this may well explain its recent increase in range. Ivy flowers in late summer and autumn and is a rich source of nectar and pollen. Almost all other bees have ceased activities when it is in flower and the most frequently seen visitors are social wasps (yellow jackets) and many kinds of fly, none of which actively collect pollen. In specializing on ivy pollen, *C. hederae* has exploited an unoccupied niche. (see Plate 2-10)

Bee species	Host plants	Lecty type	Season	Region
Colletes cunicularius	Salicaceae (Willows: *Salix* spp.)	Narrowly oligolectic	Early spring	Eurasia
C. daviesanus	Asteraceae (Daisy family)	Broadly oligolectic	Summer	Eurasia
*C. succinctus**	Ericaceae (Ling, heathers: *Calluna, Erica* spp.)	Narrowly oligolectic	Late summer	Eurasia
*C. halophilus**	Asteraceae (*Aster* spp.)	Narrowly oligolectic	Late summer	Western Europe
*C. hederae**	Araliaceae (Ivy, *Hedera helix*)	Monolectic	Late summer–autumn	Western Europe
C. nasuta	Boraginaceae (Alkanets, *Anchusa* spp.)	Narrowly oligolectic	Spring	Mediterranean, Southwest Asia

Table 1. Different levels of pollen specialization in six species of *Colletes* (plasterer bees) and their pollen sources.

*Closely related species comprising the *Colletes succinctus* species group.

In years when the flowering of ivy is late, female *C. hederae* will forage on late-flowering species of members of the daisy family, especially *Aster* species. Examples such as this have led to the suggestion that monolecty is not a useful concept. Observations that the larvae of allegedly monolectic species develop perfectly well on "alien" pollen would support this view, one that implies that there is no physiological reason why bees should be monolectic. Nevertheless, there are species which seem to be genuinely monolectic. For example, *Lasioglossum lustrans*, forages for pollen exclusively on Carolina Desert Chicory, *Pyrrhopappus carolinianus*, and in Eurasia *Andrena florea* gathers pollen only at flowers of White Bryony, *Bryonia alba*.

The relationship between flowering plants and the bees that specialize on their pollen is asymmetrical in that the plants are not dependent solely on the oligolectic bees that visit them. Exceptions are the squashes and sunflowers of the Americas, which co-evolved with their specialist bees before European settlers introduced the honeybee.

Creosote Bush (*Larrea tridentate*) is an extreme example of the asymmetry of some plant-bee relationships. This is a major landscape feature of deserts of the south-western United States and Mexico. It is self-fertile, so sets seed in the absence of pollinators and yet has a total of 96 bee species recorded as visitors, 22 of which are oligolectic.

Another way of expressing this asymmetry is to note that the presence of a given plant species is not necessarily predictive of the local presence of its oligolectic bees. If suitable nest sites are not available, then the bees may well be absent from the area. Furthermore, the climatic determinants of the distribution of plants and bees often do not always coincide. Conversely, if nest sites are available and the climate suits both plants and bees, then the presence of the plant is usually predictive of the presence of oligolectic bees associated with it.

Non-specialist bees in the pollen market sometimes major on a particularly abundant pollen and nectar source, giving the impression of oligolecty. This is a temporary situation called **flower constancy** and reflects bees' ability to detect and exploit local and temporarily abundant resources. When the flowering of such plants is over or their resources are depleted, the bees will return to being generalists.

Other forms of specialization

The females of many bee species have evolved structural adaptations which facilitate the gathering of nectar and pollen from flowers with very narrow corolla tubes. Such flowers are far too narrow for a bee to insert her head or forelegs to gain access to the pollen.

Instead, they have evolved a sort of bottle-brush tongue. Here, the outer sheath of the tongue, the galea, is covered with dense hairs, which in many species are hooked at the tip. The bee probes a flower with her long tongue and at the same time, the stiff hairs on the galea rasp pollen from the anthers. The pollen builds up between the hairs and the female uses rows of dense bristles on the underside of her foreleg to transfer the pollen in the usual way to the middle legs and then to the scopa on the hind legs.

This bottlebrush tongue seems to have evolved independently several times in long-tongued bees in apid genera such as the mining bees *Eucera* and *Anthophora*. In Israel and Palestine, I have found several species of both genera associated with the brilliant blue flowers of Prickly Alkanet, *Anchusa strigosa*.

Also oligolectic on Prickly Alkanet are females of a plasterer bee, *Colletes nasutus*. Like all species of plasterer bees, they are committed to being a short-tongued bee because it uses its short, blunt tongue as a paint brush to apply the transparent, cellophane-like lining to their brood cells. *C. nasutus* overcomes this difficulty by having a greatly elongated face. (Plate 7-2)

Instead of a greatly elongated faces, females of the southern African melittid genus *Rediviva* have greatly elongated front legs. They specialize in collecting oils from plants in the genus *Diascia*. (Plate 7-3; see also Plate 8-4)

Bees: A Natural History

Plate 7-2

Plate 7-2. Female *Colletes* are committed to being short-tongued bees because they use their blunt tongues as a kind of paint brush to apply a lining secretion to the walls of their brood cells. Females of the Eurasian *Colletes nasutus* are able to get around this limitation and gather nectar from deep-tubed flowers by having a greatly elongated head. Credit: Josef Dvořàk.

Plate 7-3

Plate 7-3. A female of the southern African melittid mining bee, *Rediviva emdeorum*. The enormously elongated front legs have specialized hairs on their feet for gathering oils from flowers of *Diascia* spp. The oil glands are at the end of two long spurs, which the bee probes with its front legs. In so doing, pollen is deposited on the bee's body. There are several species of *Diascia*, each with spurs of different lengths. There are species of *Rediviva* which have front legs of the appropriate length for the different species of *Diascia*.
Credit: Michael Kuhlmann.

Bees: A Natural History

Why specialize?

There may be risks in being a narrow specialist. So far as oligolectic bees are concerned, the risk lies in the possibility of local extinctions of their pollen sources. Any factors which threaten host plants are automatically threats to local populations of the bees. There must therefore be good reasons for evolving close associations with a pollen source.

There is evidence that there is a genetic component to oligolecty. Working with Eurasian mason bees, *Heriades truncorum*, which are oligolectic on members of the daisy family (Asteraceae), Université de Neuchâtel bee scientist Christope Praz and colleagues found unambiguous evidence that host plant recognition is genetically determined. When females in an enclosure were presented with non-host plants, they ceased nesting activities. Another part of this study showed that regardless of the pollen fed to larvae either host or non-host pollen females only foraged at their normal host plants, strong evidence that larval imprinting is not involved in host-plant choice. Furthermore, males which, as larvae, were fed only on pollen from non-host plants, restricted their mate searching to host plants.

Much further research remains to be done on oligolecty and its benefits, though there is already evidence that being a specialist confers shorter handling times at flowers. American bee ecologist, Karen Strickler studied a mason bee, *Hoplitis anthocopoides*, which makes exposed mud nests on rocks and stones. This is a Eurasian species which was accidentally introduced into North America and is now established. Females are oligolectic on Bugloss flowers, *Echium* spp. She showed that the handling times per flower by females of this bee were significantly shorter than those of five other, non-specialist bee species which visited the same plants. The rate of pollen collection was significantly greater and the amount of time spent on flowers needed to raise a single offspring was significantly smaller.

Pollen for bees is rather like crude oil is for our species. We use oil as the basic chemical resource from which we produce plastics, drugs, man-made fibers, fuels, pesticides and a whole range of other organic compounds.

For bees, the chemistry set provided by pollen includes sterols, proteins, amino acids and many other substances from which they make a wide range of hormones, a wide range of pheromones and nest lining substances, wax, royal jelly, and venoms. The basic components of all these substances can only come from pollen, so I am confident that future research will show that oligolecty and its evolution may at least in part have been driven by the chemical needs of bees and the range of chemicals to be found in pollen.

Plate 8-1

Bees and Orchids

8

An orchid in a deep forest sends out its fragrance even if no one is around to appreciate it. Likewise, men of noble character hold firm to their high principles, undeterred by poverty.

Confucius (551–479 BC)

"...the contrivances by which Orchids are fertilised, are as varied and almost as perfect as any of the most beautiful adaptations in the animal kingdom;..."

Charles Darwin (1809–1882)

On the various contrivances by which British and foreign orchids are fertilised by insects, and on the good effects of intercrossing. 1862, London: John Murray

We regard orchids as rare, exotic and charismatic plants, reserved for that special corsage or careful nurturing in a greenhouse or on a window sill. In fact, the Orchidaceae is the largest and most diverse family of flowering plants. With 22-30,000 species it accounts for 8 percent of all flowering plants. Orchids are widespread, with most species in the tropics, very many in areas with a Mediterranean-style climate. They are well-represented in temperate zones as well and a few species are even adapted to arctic conditions.

Bees have some of their most bizarre and specialized relationships with orchids. This is especially strange when one considers the way orchids present their pollen: it is enclosed in sacs, or pollinia, so this reward is not available as a collectible food resource for visiting bees.

Pollinia are often paired and are born on a stalk, the caudicle, with a sticky pad or viscidium at its base. This adheres to smooth parts of a bee's body such as the eyes, mouthparts or the rear of the thorax. The vast majority of orchids are pollinated by bees, but some specialize in exploiting raspy crickets, hawkmoths, beetles, flies and birds as pollinators.

About one third of all orchid species provide no reward at all, which makes the bee-orchid relationship seem almost perverse. The most highly evolved relationships between orchids and bees are based on

deception or what amounts to physical abuse. But still, the bees keep coming...!

Indeed, they have been coming for at least 15-20 million years. An extinct stingless bee, *Proplebeia dominicana*, was found in amber of Miocene age bearing the distinctive pollinaria (Plate 8-2) of what is the only structure available on which researchers in 2007 could base the original description of the orchid, which they named *Meliorchis caribea*. This is an extinct species, which, based on features of the pollinaria, is related to the modern tropical genera *Kreodanthus* and *Microchilus*.

This fossil bee and its pollen load are of great importance for a variety of reasons. It is the first ever fossil of an orchid, albeit of a very small fragment. It is also the first fossil evidence of a pollinator-plant relationship. Furthermore, it places the orchids further back in evolutionary time than hitherto envisaged. Because orchids are highly evolved, this fossil led its describers to postulate that orchids were extant in the late Cretaceous, 76–84 million years ago. This means that early orchids were contemporaries of the dinosaurs before the mass extinctions at the end of the Cretaceous and early Tertiary periods.

Because the pollinaria of this orchid were deployed on the rear of the bee's thorax, it is very likely that *Meliorchis caribea* had a gullet-shaped or tubular flower which the bee had to enter fully before its body came in contact with the anther bearing the pollinarium.

Despite being the most structurally diverse of all flowering plant families, the majority of orchids have a modified petal, the labellum, which acts as a landing platform for visiting bees (Plate 8-3, and Plate 8-8).

Orchid flowers are very different from typical flowers: the male and female parts are not in the form of a separate array of pollen bearing anthers and a central pistil bearing the stigma. Instead, they are fused and born on a single structure, the column. There is only one anther and this is separated from the stigma by a projection called the rostellum.

When a bee backs out after visiting an orchid flower and brushes against the anther, it dislodges the pollinia, which attach to its body via the sticky viscidium. When it next visits an orchid flower of the same species, the

Plate 8-1. The brilliantly metallic head of a male orchid bee, *Euglossa* sp. Bees in this and related genera comprise the tribe Euglossini. Both sexes are notable for their very long tongues, hence the tribal name. The males have complex and bizarre relationships with the orchids they pollinate in Central and South America (pages 138–144). Orchid bees are found from Mexico to northern Argentina. One species, *Euglossa* viridissima, was introduced into Florida and has become established. Credit: James Liebherr. (see page 132)

Plate 8-2. A fossil worker of the extinct stingless bee, *Proplebeia dominicana*, bearing pollinaria of the orchid *Meliorchis caribea*. Pollinaria are pollinia divided into many small sectional packages. (Reproduced with permission from Santiago R. Ramirez, *et al.*, 2007. *Nature* 448 : 1042–1045).

Plate 8-2

Plate 8-3

**Plate 8-3. Orchid labellum.
Pigeon orchid, *Dendrobium crumenatum*.
Credit: Guido Bohne.**

rostellum rasps against the pollinia, removing them and they then come into direct contact with the stigma, the female part of the flower and the orchid is pollinated. This mechanism operates in all orchids, whether or not they offer any kind of reward.

Orchids which offer rewards to pollinators

Some orchids which produce nectar have very tiny flowers in which the labellum is greatly reduced in size and the flowers are too small for most bees to enter. Here, the orchid deposits pollinia on the bee's tongues. The Lady's Tresses orchids (*Spiranthes* spp.) are a good example. The North American Slender Lady's Tresses (*Spiranthes gracilis*) is pollinated by solitary mining bees such as the andrenid, *Calliopsis andreniformis*, a leafcutter, *Megachile brevis*, and the American bumblebee, *Bombus americanum*. The European Autumn Lady's Tresses (*Spiranthes spiralis*) is pollinated by bumblebees.

The large showy Neotropical "Queen of Orchids" (*Cattleya* spp.) produces nectar at the base of a deep spur and are therefore pollinated by long-tongued bees such as species of the large orchid bees, *Eulaema* or giant carpenter bees, *Xylocopa* spp. Others are pollinated by bumblebees.

The bees' probing movements dislodge the pollinia, which adhere to the rear of the thorax.

In both the summer and winter rainfall areas of South Africa, there is a complex of four related orchids: Shield (*Ceratandra*, 1 sp.), Monkshood (*Corycium*, 4 spp.), Disperis (*Disperis*, 12 spp.), and Ground (*Pterygodium*, 13 spp.). All produce oils as a reward. In this, they resemble the Twinspur (*Diascia* spp.) and Monkey Face (*Hemimeris* spp.) discussed in the last chapter. The resemblance extends to the solitary bees which pollinate them, species of *Rediviva*, which have elongate front legs with which to harvest nectar from the twin spurs of the *Diascia* species (see Plate 7-3). The distribution of the orchids broadly overlaps with that of the bees.

The species within each of these orchid genera are very closely related and, by means of differences in their anatomy, each species deposits its pollinia on a different part of the body of visiting female *Rediviva* spp. In this way, local populations of co-occurring orchid species can share a limited pool of specialised pollinators, without hybridisation or wasteful deposition of pollinia in flowers of the wrong species. In other words, the orchids maintain reproductive isolation by mechanical means.

By evolving the secretion of oils, these orchids have bought into the pollination network which includes plants from a different family, the Scrophulariaceae. Thus at the broad regional level, a total 33 orchid species and about 70 species of *Diascia* and 5 species of *Hemimeris* have access to the pollinating services of eight species of specialist, oil-collecting bees (*Rediviva* spp.).

At the level of the local population, however, only a subsection of the total orchid-bee guild occurs. The different species of *Rediviva* bees have different nest site preferences based on soil texture, so are not evenly distributed across their range. Thus, their distribution is a geographic mosaic pattern reflecting the distribution of different patterns of soil texture. The orchid species have different but adjoining (= parapatric) distributions, with only marginal overlap.

In the coastal lowlands of the Western Cape Province of South Africa the local oil-producing plants comprise fifteen species of orchid, several species of *Diascia* and the Bobbejaangesiggies (*Hemimeris racemosa*) plus *Rediviva peringueyi*. Together they form a pollination guild, the orchids having little interaction with other *Rediviva* species.

DNA studies of pollinaria removed from the bees indicated that the orchid species have only recently diverged from a common ancestor; they differ in the site of pollinia attachment and so reproductive isolation by mechanical means is an early feature of species diversification (Plates 8-4).

Cheats sometimes prosper

The European Green-winged orchid, *Anacamptis morio* (formerly known as *Orchis morio*) is pollinated by bumblebees, *Bombus* spp. This orchid produces no nectar and a study in Sweden showed that the visitation and therefore pollination rate is greatly enhanced when the orchid grows in the vicinity of nectar producing species such as the Water Aven (*Geum rivale*) and Wild Chive (*Allium schoenoprasum*).

The orchid relies, therefore, on the energetic investment made by other species in producing nectar to attract pollinators into their vicinity. Energy saving in this way is also seen in two South American species of *Cattleya*, the long-stalked *C. elongate* and slender-stemmed *C. tenuata*. They have given up nectar production and rely on the probing movements by queens of the neotropical bumblebee *Bombus brevivillus* to detach their pollinia, which become stuck to the rear of the bee's thorax.

These two orchids are true cheats: like the nectar producing species of *Cattleya*, they use scent to attract the bees. They rely on the fact that neighboring species of *Cattleya*, which produce nectar, provide bees with a learning experience which leads them to associate a particular flower structure with a nectar reward. By the time they discover that there is no nectar it is too late: the bees have either picked up or deposited pollinia and the cheating *Cattleya* species have saved energy by not producing nectar.

Orchid bees of the new world tropics: scented oils as a reward for male bees

In the tropics and subtropics of Central and South America, a group of about 200 bee species and about 400 orchids have co-evolved in such a way as to intertwine their sex-lives in a network of bizarre relationships. This network is not only key to their own reproductive success, but also to that of the forests as a whole and in ways which are of direct and great economic importance to humans.

The bees involved are commonly called orchid bees, whose closest relatives are the bumblebees. It is the males of these bees which have highly specialized relationships with orchids (Plate 8-5) and it is the females which are such important pollinators of forest trees. Together with honeybees and stingless bees, they are often referred to as corbiculate bees, that is, the females and workers have pollen baskets or corbiculae for the transport of pollen back to the nest. (see Chapter 2 and 4; Plates 4-2 and 8-5) These bees belong to the tribe Euglossini, a name which indicates that these bees have very long tongues, sometimes up to 4cm (1.5 inches). There are five genera: *Eulaema* and *Eufriesia*, which resemble large, robust, furry bumblebees and three brilliantly shining and metallic genera, *Euglossa*, *Aglae*, and *Exaerete*. The last two genera are cuckoos in the nests of other euglossines.

Unlike the deceptive bee orchids (*Ophrys* spp., see144-147), the orchids which have invested their sexual success in male orchid bees actually produce an attractive reward-scent. The males collect and store these scents and have evolved a suite of structural features which enable them to handle and, ultimately, deploy them for their own purposes.

The 400 or so orchid species which are exclusively pollinated by male euglossines belong to two closely related subfamilies, the Stanhopeinae and Catasetinae.

These most specialized of orchids do not make it easy for the bees to harvest the scents. In fact, they put the males through some sort of physical ordeal which, as we shall see, may well have significance later in the sexual activities of the bees.

The ordeals usually involve some sort of trap mechanism. While the bee is trapped, the orchid flower cements its pair of pollinia to the bee's body. This is important: when the male next visits another flower of the same orchid species, the pollinia are correctly placed to be received by the receptive female part of the flower. Closely related orchid species avoid wasteful hybridizations by this simple but effective mechanical means of reproductive isolation. (Plate 8-7)

Morm orchids (*Mormodes* spp.) use one of the simplest trap mechanisms. While scrabbling for scent droplets on the surface of the orchid, a male euglossine eventually arrives at a specialized petal called the labellum. A structure called the column reacts by pressing down on the bee, trapping it against the labellum.

Bees: A Natural History

Plate 8-4

R. neliana

C. dracomontanum pollinaria

P. cooperi pollinaria

R. longimanus

P. pentherianum pollinaria

P. schelpei pollinaria

Plate 8-4. A: A female *Rediviva brunnea* collects oil from the orchid *Pterygonium magnum*. **B:** Different orchid species, *Pterygonium cooperi* and *Corycium dracomontanum*, deposit their pollinaria on different parts of a bee's body. (Photographs © Anton Pauw, reproduced with permission from Waterman, R. J., et al., 2011. *The American Naturalist* 177(2): E54–E68).

The paired pollinia, produced at the end of the column, are applied to the rear of the bee's thorax. The flower traps the bee long enough for cement produced at the base of the pollinia to dry.

Charles Darwin observed euglossine males at *Mormodes* orchids and described their behavior. However, as with *Ophrys* orchids (see below), he thought they were females and could not understand what attracted the bees to flowers which produce no nectar and whose pollen was unusable.

The 11 species of Bucket orchid, *Coryanthes* spp., use a rather more intriguing mechanism. Here, the labellum is massively produced to form a bucket-shaped structure. This receives droplets of water from a pair of faucets at the base of the column. When a male euglossine lands on the rim of the bucket, he finds an area of glandular tissue which produces an oily scent, which he collects. Eventually he strays on to an area of slippery cells and falls into the water in the bucket.

The only way he can gain purchase on the sides of the bucket in his attempts to escape is along a vertical tract where the surface is rougher than elsewhere. This directs him to where the front edge of the bucket is produced into a spout. Just as he reaches this position, down drops the column, where he may be trapped for up to 40 minutes by, *Coryanthes speciosa*, during which time the pollinia are glued to the base of his abdomen (Plate 8-5); other species of bucket orchid detain the bee for shorter periods.

Plate 8-6

euglossine displays are correct, but there are still gaps in our knowledge.

The facts of life as they pertain to the sexual networks of euglossine bees and orchids are not merely interesting facets of natural history. These bees and orchids occupy keystone positions in sustaining the forests of the tropical Americas. Female euglossines, together with other large bees, are the principle pollinators of economically important trees such as the Brazil Nut (*Bertholletia excelsa*). Forest trees such as this depend on the long-distance pollinating services of bees.

Unlike the typical temperate forest, tropical forests have high species *diversity* with corresponding low species *density*. A typical Amazonian forest tree may be separated by 1–3km (0.6-1.9 miles) from its nearest conspecific neighbor, which means that any pollinating bees must be able to fly at least this distance. In fact, both sexes of euglossines have been shown to be

capable of long foraging flights, no doubt aided by the ability to fly at speeds of 5m/sec. This would enable them to cover 50km (31 miles) in just less than three hours and some females are believed regularly to fly up to 20km (12 miles) on a foraging trip.

The epiphytic orchids whose scents support the sex lives of euglossine bees do not grow on Brazil Nut trees, so here we have what appears to be a counter-intuitive situation: the valuable Brazil nut crop is at least partially dependent on the reproductive success of both epiphytic orchids and the male bees which pollinate them but which never visit Brazil nut flowers.

Apart from female euglossines, a Brazil nut blossom is pollinated by large bees such as giant carpenter bees, *Xylocopa* spp., and bees of the oil-collecting genera *Centris* and *Epicharis*. Females of these bees collect oils from the flowers of lianas and trees in the family Malphigiaceae.

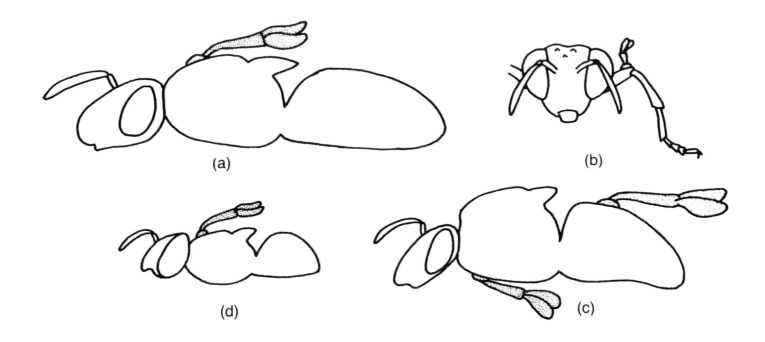

(a)

(b)

(d)

(c)

Plate 8-7

Plate 8-7. Diagrammatic outlines of male euglossine bees showing the precise positioning of pollinia by five species of *Catasetum* orchids. (a) pollinia of *Catasetum macrocarpum* on *Eulaema meriana*; (b) pollinia of two species of *Catasetum* on *Eulaema meriana*; (c) that of *Catasetum saccatum* on upper surface of abdomen, that of *C. discolour* on underside of thorax; (d) pollinia of *Catasetum barbatum* on *Euglossa cordata*. Redrawn after Dressler, R. L., 1967, *Evolution* 22: 202–210 and reproduced from Christopher O'Toole. and Anthony Raw 1991. *Bees of the World*. Blandford–Cassell. 192pp.

Thus, the pollination success for this important crop depends also on the presence and successful pollination of oil producing species. This is yet another powerful argument for conserving the diversity of tropical American forests.

Bolivia is the world's largest producer of shelled Brazil nuts, an industry which employs up to 100,000 jobs either directly or indirectly, supporting 28,000 families which depend on it for their income. So the arguments for conserving biodiversity and using it sustainably are profoundly economic, not merely the romantic yearnings of nature lovers.

Bee orchids and sexual deception

Bee orchids (*Ophrys* spp.) are so-called because the labellum of each species is said to resemble the female of a solitary bee. This notion was established when it became apparent to naturalists that only male bees visited the flowers. (Plate 8-8)

Charles Darwin was particularly bemused by these orchids. He wrote his great book on the pollination mechanisms of orchids before it was established that only male bees visited the bee orchids. He thought that the visitors were females and, knowing that the orchids produced no attractive rewards, was puzzled that such "intelligent" insects should be so easily fooled.

Ophrys is most diverse in the Mediterranean region, with endemic species on several islands. Several species occur north of the Alps and there are four species native to Britain. At the time of writing, there is debate and disagreement between researchers as to the exact number of species. The issue is complicated by the fact that these orchids are popular with amateur plant taxonomists with a stamp-collector obsession with describing new species, subspecies and varieties in journals, which do not operate a system of peer

Plate 8-8. A male long-horned bee, *Eucera vulpes*, approaching a bee orchid flower, *Ophrys helenae*. The large lower petal is the labellum. Paliouri, Greece. Credit: Nicolas J. Vereecken.

Bees: A Natural History

Plate 8-8

Plate 8–9

The importance of bee–orchid guilds

Apart from their intrinsic interest, the many bee-orchid pollination guilds are potent examples of just how complex the relationships are between insects and the other organisms with which they interact. Because of their visual appeal and impact, bees and their pollinating relationships with plants have iconic status and are now being studied more intensively than ever.

We need to understand the complex network of mutually sustaining relationships between organisms. Fortunately, we know something of the euglossine-orchid-Brazil nut story; these bees, because of their long distance foraging capabilities and their important contribution to the maintenance of neotropical forest habitats, are now recognized as important bio-indicators of the health of tracts of forest. But how many other such networks remain to be discovered? Are we really yet in a position to decide what are the minimal sustainable sizes of protected habitats?

And why should clock and watchmakers be concerned that the complex pollination scenario of the Brazil nut be sustained? Brazil nut oil is their lubricant of choice.

Plate 8-9. A male *Megachile parietina* pseudocopulating with a bee orchid flower, *Ophrys ferrum*. A male in the background has a pair of pollinia stuck to his head, indicating that he has already visited another bee orchid. Vassilopoulo, Greece. Credit: Nicolas J. Vereecken.

Plate 9-1

The Enemies of Bees

9

Although flowers provide bees with their food resources, they can be dangerous places. Crab spiders lurk and pounce, some species being protected from detection by their chameleon-like ability to change color to match their background. (see Plate 9-1) Floral dangers also include assassin bugs, members of the true bug order Hemiptera. These predators use their long, penetrating proboscis to inject digestive fluids into their prey and then to imbibe a pre-digested meal. (Plate 9-2) Praying mantis are also a risk factor in many parts of the world. (Plate 9-3)

Recent research has shown that honeybees have evolved a defensive response to these flower-based enemies: if they survive an attack, they mark the flower with an alarm pheromone, a warning scent which deters hive-mates from visiting it.

In North America, the northern mockingbird (*Mimus polyglottos*) also includes bees as part of its diet. And even though honeybees are not native to the Americas, skunks have developed a ploy for preying on them: they scrape the side of wooden beehives and catch defending bees which emerge. The skunks seem oblivious to being stung.

These predators are opportunist feeders: bees are not their only prey. There are, however, some predators which specialize on bees and wasps. Among birds, the brightly-colored bee-eaters comprise a family of 26 species found in Eurasia, Africa and Australasia.

Plate 9-1. A crab spider, *Misumenia vatia*, with its honeybee worker prey. This spider is found across North America and Europe and can change color to match that of the flowers on which it waits for visiting prey. This individual clearly didn't have time to change its color. Credit: Charles Krebs. (see page 150)

Plate 9-2. An assassin bug (Hemiptera: Reduviidae) sucking the body fluids of it prey, a stingless bee, *Trigona* sp. Penang Hill, Malaya. Credit: Edward Ross.

Plate 9-2

Plate 9-3

They seek prey on the wing, darting out from a regular perch. Honeybees comprise about one third of their prey.

The hunting wasps called bee-wolves are rather more specialized. *Philanthus gibbosus*, for example, is a North American species which preys on sweat bees. The female wasp catches bees, stinging them into paralysis and storing them in their brood cells excavated in the ground. The female provides each cell with several bees and lays an egg on one of them. Her larva feeds on the bees. The Eurasian species, *P. triangulum*, is the best known of the bee-wolves: it preys on worker honeybees Ironically, *Philanthus* species belong to the family Crabronidae, which may well have given rise to the bees (see Chapter 1).

Mites are often nest associates of bees, usually living as harmless scavengers, feeding on pollen remains and the faecal pellets of bee larvae. Sometimes the mites undergo a population explosion and they eat the pollen en masse, starving the bee larvae. Mason bees (*Osmia* species) often suffer in this way. The bees themselves unwittingly help disperse the mites, species of *Chaetodactylus*; when newly adult bees emerge from their natal nests, they bite their way through badly infested cells on their way to the exit and become infested themselves, often carrying hundreds or thousands of mites on their bodies. Some mites leave the bee each time it visits a flower, they then hitch a ride on other visiting *Osmia* and in this way the mites are spread into new nests. Mites are also spread venereally (Plate 9-4).

Some mites, such as the notorious *Varroa destructor*, are direct parasites, feeding on the blood of both larval and adult honeybees and are an economically important pest of the beekeeping industry. (Plate 9-5) Not all mites, however, are pests of bees. The females of some Carpenter bees (*Xylocopa* spp.) have a symbiotic relationship with the mite genus *Dinogamasus*. The mites live in a pouch in the front of the first abdominal segment of the bee. At night, when the bee is at rest in its nest, the mites leave the pouch and scavenge on pollen remaining on the dorsal surface of the bee. Carpenter bees have short legs and the mites groom the parts of the body the bees cannot reach for themselves.

Mason bees (*Osmia* spp.) often nest in old beetle borings in dead wood (Chapters 3 and 10). This means they often come into contact with beetles which live in this habitat, normally feeding as scavengers on the faecal pellets of the wood borer beetles. The beetles, species of *Ptinus* and *Megatoma*, often scavenge in artificial nests deployed for mason bees. Here, both adults and larvae feed on the faecal pellets of the bee larvae and the remains of pollen, acting as scavengers, especially if the beetles enter the bee nests towards the end of the bees' larval development. If they find the nests a little earlier, then they feed on the pollen, competing with the bee larvae. In such cases, the immature bees are starved to death, especially if beetle numbers are high. I have found, however, with both the North American Blue Orchard bee (*Osmia lignaria*) and the Eurasian Red Mason Bee (*O. rufa*), that sometimes the bee larvae manage to survive infestations of *Ptinus*, but the resulting adult bees are dwarves.

More specialized enemies of solitary bees include a wide range of insects with behavior that is adapted to that of their bee victims. These include flies and parasitic wasps. They seek and find the nests of bees and wait for the female bee to leave on a foraging trip. They then enter the nest and lay their eggs on the stored pollen. The eggs hatch when the bee has completed the pollen store, laid her single egg and sealed the brood cell. The larvae then feed voraciously on the pollen, and the bee larva does not survive.

Satellite flies have this life-style. They belong to the flesh fly family, the appropriately-named Sarcophagidae, most of which lay their eggs in corpses and are of interest to forensic entomologists because the rate of larval development provides information on the likely time of death of murder victims. Satellite flies, *Senotania* spp., are so-called because the females follow bees returning to the nests, shadowing them at a distance of 10–15cm (4-6 inches) and alight at the nest entrance, where they wait for the bee to leave on her next foraging trip. They enter the nest and lay their eggs.

All of these insects with larvae that feed on the stored pollen of their bee hosts are termed **cleptoparasites**.

Another group of flies, the bee-flies, in the family *Bombyliidae*, are so-called because they resemble bees. Solitary mining bees, especially species of *Andrena*, are the hosts of species of *Bombylius*. The females of these flies have a rapid darting flight and hover low off the ground where the bees nest, scattering their eggs like seeds. The eggs hatch rapidly and crawl into the bee nests, where they invade open, incomplete cells. Here, they feed on the bee larvae, eventually killing them. Insects such as these, together with the thousands of parasitic wasps, whose larvae eventually kill their hosts, are called **parasitoids**. (Plate 9-6)

Mason bees are susceptible to several such parasitoids wasps. The fact that in North America, *Osmia lignaria* and *O. rufa* share one of these wasps reflects their close relationship. The wasp concerned is *Monodontomerus obscurus*. (Plate 9-7 and Plate 9-8)

Oil beetles are so-called because they exude an oily, corrosive defensive secretion from between their leg joints when attacked. They belong to the family Meloidae and the larvae of most species are parasitoids on the larvae of bees. Just how the oil beetle larvae get into the nests of their hosts is a remarkable example of complex, highly adaptive behavior.

The female beetle lays a clutch of eggs on a flower. These hatch into larvae, often colored bright red or

Plate 9-3. Praying mantis eats a bumblebee after decapitating it. Credit: Edward Ross.

Plate 9-4

Plate 9-5

orange, with strong, clawed legs. When a bee visits the flower, they climb on to it *en masse*, clinging on to the bee's body hairs. The bee transports the larvae back to the nest. If the bee is a male, the larvae transfer to a female when she mates. Sometimes, the beetle larvae attach themselves to a cuckoo bee (see page 161) and, in the case of a male cuckoo bee, they will eventually hitch a ride on a female cuckoo bee after mating and thus gain entry into a host nest. (Plate 9-9)

In at least one species, the group of oil-beetle larvae produces a pheromone which mimics that of the sex pheromone of the female host species. When a male attempts to mate with the beetle larvae, they attach themselves to his body and transfer to his next female mate.

Inside the nest, the oil-beetle larva remains quiescent inside the bee larva until the host has grown in size. It then molts its tough cuticle, loses its legs and becomes soft-bodied, a process called **hypermetamorphosis**; it then starts to eat the bee larva, eventually killing it.

Plate 9-4. Mating pair of European Red Mason bees, *Osmis rufa*, both covered with hundreds of the mite *Chaetodactylus osmiae*. Credit: Robin Williams.

Plate 9-5. The parasitic mite, *Varroa destructor*, on a honeybee pupa. This species was accidentally introduced into populations of the Western honeybee from one of the oriental species. It causes great economic damage to beekeeping in the United States and Europe. Credit: Éric Toruneret.

Plate 9-6. The larva of a Zombie fly, *Apocephalus borealis*, emerges from the dead body of a host honeybee. The fly deposits its eggs in the abdomens of honeybees, bumblebees and wasps. As the larvae grow, within the body of the bee, the bee begins to lose control of its ability to walk, flying blindly toward light. It eventually dies and the fly larvae emerge and pupate. The fly is suspected of contributing to the decrease in honeybee populations. Credit: John Hafernik.

Plate 9-6

Plate 9-7. A female parasitoid wasp, *Monodontomerus obscurus,* has died after using her long ovipositor to inject eggs into the pupal cocoon of the Red Mason bee, *Osmia rufa.* Leicestershire, England. Credit: Christopher O'Toole.

Mining bees in the genus *Andrena* are frequently affected by parasitoids belonging to the order Strepsiptera, which have some of the most bizarre life-cycles. The name means "twisted wings" and refers to the hind wing of the male when in flight; females are wingless and live their entire lives within the bodies of their hosts, with the head protruding between two abdominal segments (Plate 9-10).

There are about 600 species worldwide and their hosts, according to species, are mainly planthoppers and bees and wasps, but solitary mining bees, especially *Andrena* species are frequently affected in both North America and Eurasia. As with oil beetles, the foraging female bees pick up the tiny strepsipteran larvae at flowers.

On arrival at the nest, the larvae wait until the bee larva is well grown. The parasite larvae secrete an enzyme which softens the cuticle of the bee larva, enabling them to penetrate the body cavity. As with oil beetles, the strepsipteran larva molts its horny cuticle, loses its legs and becomes soft-bodied and maggot-like, feeding on the tissues of the bee larva.

The bee completes it development, though and, shortly after it becomes adult, the strepsipteran larva pupates and completes its own development. If it is a male, then the pupa protrudes between two of the bee's abdominal segments and the adult male emerges. Male have two pairs of wings, the front pair are reduced and club-like.

Adult female strepsipterans are wingless and remain larviform, with the head protruding as in Plate 9-10. Unlike the males, they never leave the host. Meanwhile the infected bee feeds at flowers. If it is a female, it does not nest. The presence of these parasites during the bee's development causes profound changes. The adult bees are sterile, a phenomenon known as **parasitic castration**. There may also be other changes in the bees's body: secondary sexual characters may be reversed, so for example, females may develop the pale facial markings

Plate 9-7

Plate 9-8

characteristic of males and males may develop with female features, and the density and coarseness of body hairs may be altered.

Female strepsipterans emit a pheromone which attracts males to an infected bee. The females have no functional genital opening and the male uses a sharp, curved penis as a kind of hypodermic to inject sperm into the exposed part of the female.

Fertilised eggs hatch into as many as two thousand tiny larve, which develop by feeding within the female's body on her tissues. The larvae escape via a passage on the underside of the female's body and attach themselves to the hairs of the bee.

When the bee visits flowers the strepsipteran larvae drop off and wait for other female bees to arrive and transport them back to their nests and the cycle starts anew. (Plate 9-10)

Cuckoo bees are so-called because, like their avian namesakes, they do not makes nests. Instead, they lay their eggs in the nests of other bees. In so doing, they have no need to collect pollen and thus have lost all pollen-gathering structures such as the scopa or corbiculum.

Plate 9-8. Eight full-grown larvae of a parasitoid wasp, *Monodontomerus obscurus*, in the pupal cocoon of the Blue Orchard bee, *Osmia lignaria*. It takes 10-15 foraging trips to gather enough pollen to be converted into an orchard bee and one bee pupa to support the development of 4-15 wasps. Kern County, California. Credit: Christopher O'Toole.

Plate 9-9. A female cuckoo bee, *Nomada* sp., its thorax, abdomen and leg covered with red larvae of an oil beetle, *Meloe* sp. The larvae hitch a ride directly into the nest of the mining bee host of the *Nomada*, a species of *Andrena*. Szeged, Hungary. Credit: Henrik Gyurkovics.

Bees: A Natural History

Plate 9-9

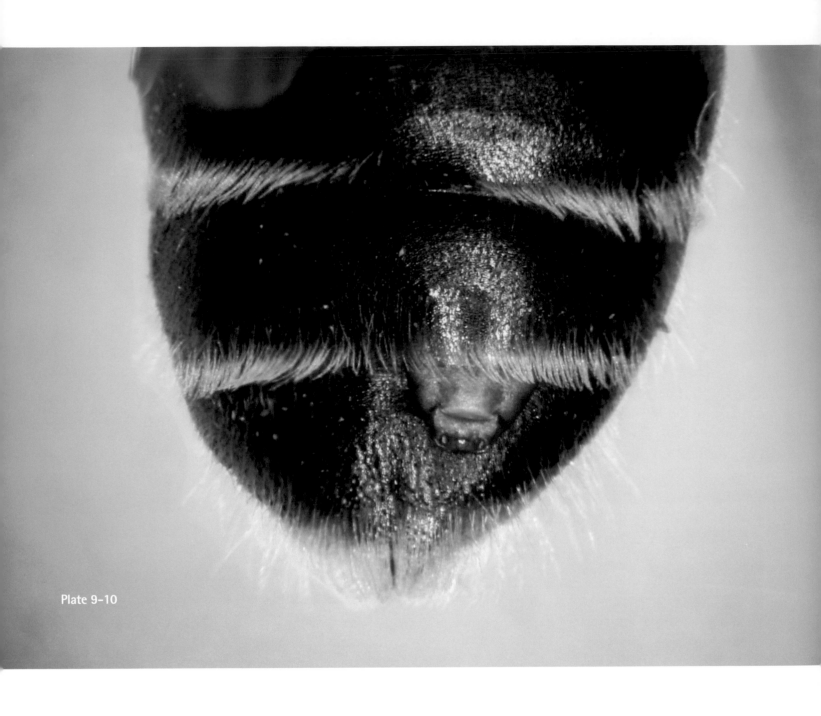

Plate 9–10

Of the 20,000 or so species of bee, 2,500 are cuckoos and four of the seven families of bees contain genera which are cuckoos. One whole apid subfamily, the Nomadinae, accounts for 1,300 species and its genus *Nomada* has more than 800 species, most of which are cuckoos in the nests of the solitary mining bee genus *Andrena*. The males of some *Nomada* species have been shown to produce a mandibular gland scent which mimics the nest marking scents of their female hosts.

This confers a double advantage: the males patrol nest areas of hosts, increasing their attractiveness to females of their own sex and enhancing their own chances of mating success, as well as aiding potential mates to find a population of their host species.

Cuckoo bees are usually fairly host specific, exploiting one or only a few closely related species.

As with the non-bee cleptoparasites mentioned previously, female cuckoo bees seek out nests of their hosts and wait for the female bee to leave the nest on a foraging trip before entering the nest and laying an egg. The egg usually hatches after the host female has completed and sealed the brood cell. The first stage larva of very many cuckoo bees has large, sickle-shaped jaws with which it destroys the host's egg or young larva.

With this task complete, the cuckoo larva molts and in so doing loses its large jaws; it now has the small jaws typical of bee larvae and feeds on the stored cell provisions.

The females of some adult cuckoo bees also have a structural modification which is an adaptation to the cuckoo life-style: those of the genus *Coelioxys* and related genera have a blade-like pointed tip to the abdomen with which they penetrate the sealed cells of their hosts. *Coelioxys* spp. makes incisions in the seals of cells of leafcutter bees, *Megachile species*.

The bumblebees genus, *Bombus*, contains a subgenus, *Psithyrus*, comprising 29 species which are cuckoos in the nests of other bumblebee species. A female enters a bumblebee colony and lurks for some time in a crevice at the bottom of the nest, absorbing its scent. The workers thus regard the interloper as a nest mate and ignore her.

The female cuckoo eats the eggs laid by the colony queen and substitutes her own eggs. Very often, the cuckoo kills the host queen and takes over the colony, exploiting the host workers, who gather pollen and nectar and rear her offspring.

It might seem that bees are beleagured by a range of enemies, but they now have contend with a newcomer our own species.

Plate 9–10. The abdomen of a female solitary mining bee, *Andrena chrysosceles*, with the head of a female *Strepsipteran*, protruding from between segments 5 and 6. Bees thus affected are said to be stylopized. Leicestershire, England. Credit: Christopher O'Toole.

Plate 10-1

The Conservation and Management of Bees

10

It is ironic that the pollinating success of four bumblebee species in New Zealand, together with Britain's long-term shaky relationship with France, would eventually lead to the decline of wild bees in Britain.

Bumblebees are not native to New Zealand and were introduced in order to pollinate clover and alfalfa (lucerne). These are important forage crops for cattle and sheep.

Unfortunately, the native bee fauna of New Zealand comprises only 28 species, all with short tongues and incapable of pollinating these crops. The honeybee had been introduced many years previously but this species is not an efficient pollinator of these vital crops: they tend to avoid contact with sexual parts of alfalfa flowers and gain access to nectaries by biting holes at the base of the flower.

The bumblebees were introduced into New Zealand in 1885 and again in 1906. The species were the Garden (*Bombus hortorum*), Large Garden (*B. ruderatus*), Short-haired (*B. subterraneus*) and Buff-tailed (*B. terrestris*) bumblebees. (see Plates 10-1, 10-2, 10-3 and 10-8)

They became established and were a great success. This was the first time bees other than honeybees were introduced to another country as pollinators. It was potent proof that having the right bees in the right place at the right time can have profound effects on agriculture: within a few years, New Zealand went from being an annual importer of clover seed to being a net exporter. Furthermore, the pollination services of the bumblebees enabled New Zealand to nurture a highly efficient cattle, sheep and dairy products industry.

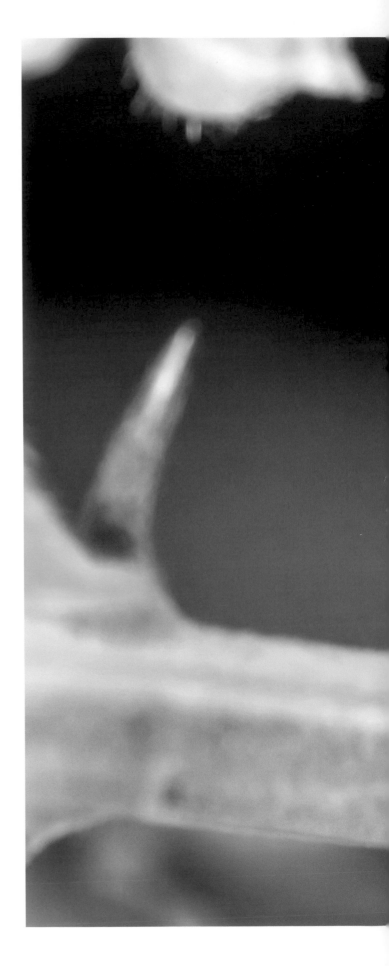

Plate 10-1. The Large Garden bumblebee, *Bombus hortorum*, is one of four species introduced into New Zealand. Credit: Henk Wallays. (see page 164)

Plate 10-2. A worker Short-haired bumblebee, *Bombus subterraneaus*. This species was introduced into New Zealand in the 19th century from Britain, where it is now extinct. Swedish bees were re-introduced back into Britain in 2012. Credit: Nikos Tsatsakis.

Bees: A Natural History

Plate 10-2

The first large scale use of these bees began more than fifty years ago in Japan, involving the Horn-faced Mason bee (*Osmia cornifrons*) for apple pollination. This species frequently nests in reed stems and apple farmers have been in the habit of gathering occupied nests and placing them in their orchards. About 70 percent of Japan's apple crop is pollinated by this bee and it is also an effective pollinator of pears and is also managed as a pollinator in China and Korea. Research has shown that the Horn-faced Mason bee is 80 times more effective at pollinating apples than honeybees; it has been used in Pennsylvania for apple pollination and has become established in several US states.

A native North American mason bee, the Blue Orchard (*Osmia lignaria*), is also an effective pollinator of spring-flowering rosaceous crops—almonds, apples, cherries, pears and plums. (Plate 10-6) Blue Orchard bees can be mass reared in enclosures to provide pollinating populations for orchards: cocoons are over-wintered in cool room at 4°C (39.2°F) and can then be incubated appropriately for their mass emergence in orchards of the target crops. The bees use artificial nests placed in the orchards. (Plate 10-7)

In Europe, the Red Mason bee, *Osmia rufa*, and Horned Mason bee, *O. cornuta,* are known to be good pollinators of these crops, together with strawberries in greenhouses and polytunnels. Red Mason bees are now increasingly used for apple pollination in south east Poland. Table 10-2 lists the Mason bee species (*Osmia*) which are used as managed pollinators or which have potential.

Plate 10–5. An Australian apid mining bee, *Amegilla asserta,* approaches a tomato flower, *Solanum lycopersicum,* in a hothouse. This species has potential as a commercial pollinator. Credit: Anne and Les Dollin/Australian Native Bee Research Centre.

Bees: A Natural History

Plate 10–5

Plate 10-6

Bees: A Natural History

It is clear that agriculture needs to broaden its pollinator base and not rely on the honeybee as the sole managed species. This is achieved by harnessing knowledge of the nesting biology of solitary bees and the relationships with flowering plants. Wild pollinators, however, need conserving and this is increasingly difficult in the face of intensive agricultural practices.

When I was involved in the development in California of the native Blue Orchard bee as a managed pollinator of almonds, I placed trap-nests in three localities in Kern County. These were deployed from 2006 to 2009. Not one was ever occupied. One of the sites was in the Kern County Nature Preserve.

I also tried to interest some growers in providing suitable bee forage plants in marginal areas close to almond orchards. The idea was to provide extra resources for both honeybees and Blue Orchard bees to keep them going after the end of the short blooming period of almonds—three to four weeks depending on variety. I was unsuccessful; but where I failed, the Xerces Society has been successful and trials are now underway in which extra forage is being planted close to some orchards. Initial results show that adding forage crops in and around almond orchards improves the health of honeybee colonies. Hopefully, this practice will also aid the recovery of native bees.

In order to co-ordinate research on the status of the more than 2,500 European bee species and other pollinators in the agricultural landscape, the European Union (EU) has started an international initiative STEP (Status and Trends of European Pollinators). This is a partnership of 19 countries, the largest ever coordinated project on bee diversity and pollination.

One important aim here is to raise awareness among farmers of the importance of wild pollinators. This is important because one of STEP's early findings confirms what many had suspected for some time: the number of honeybees in some parts of Europe is now insufficient

Plate 10-6. Female Blue Orchard bees, *Osmia lignaria*, at Scorpion weed, *Phacelia tanacetifolia*, in a mass rearing enclosure in California's San Joaquin Valley. Credit: Christopher O'Toole.

Plate 10-7

Plate 10-7. A trial nest unit for Blue Orchard bees, *Osmia lignaria*, in an almond orchard. Kern County, California. Credit: Christopher O'Toole.

Plate 10-8. A queen Large Garden bumblebee, *Bombus hortorum*, uses her very long tongue to probe for nectar in a flower of *Rhododendron ponticum*. She has just emerged from winter hibernation and is refueling while on her search for a suitable nest site. The nectar of *Rhododendron* contains toxic alkaloids which renders honey derived from this source poisonous to humans. Bees, however, seem unaffected. Scotland. Credit: Christopher O'Toole.

Plate 10-8

The Conservation and Management of Bees

Plate 10–9

Plate 10–9. Owing to the lack of bees, Chinese farmers have resorted to pollinating their orchards by hand. Credit: Li junsheng / Imaginechina.

Bees: A Natural History

to provide adequate pollination services. A STEP-related study in Britain showed that honeybees pollinate only a third of insect-pollinated crops; bumblebees, solitary bees and, to a lesser extent, hoverflies are the principal pollinators.

Farmers, especially orchard growers, whether they realize it or not, now increasingly depend on wild bees. Unfortunately, the diversity of wild bees in Europe is in decline. Records of more than 32 million pollinators and plants lead to this conclusion; not only is there a reduction in bee diversity, at the level of the local population, there is evidence that the species composition is becoming more uniform.

If this trend continues, then European agriculture faces the prospect of a major pollination deficit, with decreased yields of many fruit and vegetables. Pollinators are vital for 84 percent of the 150 crops grown in Europe, which have a total annual value of $28.7 billion (£17.85 billion; €22 billion). The value of the honeybee's contribution to this is estimated to be 30–50 times the value of the honey crop and wax production.

STEP is a laudable enterprise. However, growing problems with the conservation of bees and the habitats they both support and depend on are global and thus require global initiatives. Fortunately, one such initiative has been proposed following a pilot study funded by the Food and Agriculture Organization of the United Nations. The study used seven different sampling methods in three continents (Brazil, Ghana, Kenya, South Africa, India, Nepal, and Pakistan). The proposal suggests that paid workers around the world use "pan traps" in which bees are attracted to brightly-colored pans filled with liquid. They would identify and count the bees. The 200–250 sampling locations each sampled twice over 5 years would provide sufficient data to detect small (2–5 percent) annual declines in the number of species and total abundance.

This would cost U.S.$2 million, which is a very small sum compared to the more than $200 billion/year which is the annual value of pollination services provided mainly by bees. To this must be added the inestimable value of the pollination services provided by bees in maintaining habitats and landscapes to which we accord recreational and aesthetic importance.

Our species clearly has a vested interest in knowing as much as possible about as many bee species as we can if we are to recruit more pollinators and conserve them and their habitats.

The mutual dependence of bees and flowering plants has a long history. Each has contributed to the making of the other's diversity over many millions of years, an example of co-evolution that is of more than passing interest to humankind: it all boils down to biodiversity and maintaining the network of life-sustaining networks on which all species depend.

There are now too many stark examples of network failure: there are vast orchards in Sichuan Province, China, where the over use of insecticides has virtually eliminated pests. This policy was intended to increase fruit yields but had the opposite effect: it eliminated the pollinating bees. The result is that each spring, 40,000 people now have the job of pollinating the fruit trees by hand, using feather dusters. (Plate 10-9)

Biodiversity is the long-term bank account from which we are in danger of increasing our overdraft beyond sustainable levels.

Plate 11-1

Bees and People

11

Bees: A Natural History

Plate 11-2

The bee is small among the fowles, yet doth its fruite pass in sweetness.

Ecclesiastes XI 3 (Translation of 1603)

Perhaps it is because humans are social animals that we are fascinated by bees. The honeybee has always had a prominence in human affairs which far exceeds its roles as pollinator and source of useful products. Wherever people have come into contact with bees, there is virtually no culture or major religion in which the bee does not have magical or mystical significance.

The earliest record of human association with bees is a Palaeolithic cave painting in the mountains of eastern Spain. It shows people robbing nests in a rock cleft. The practise of robbing the nests of wild honeybee colonies, or those of stingless bees, persists to this day, and probably stems from pre-human times, for our close relatives, the chimpanzee and orangutan, occasionally rob nests for honey and bee grubs.

The large honey stores of the highly social bees made it worthwhile for people to attempt exploitation, and true beekeeping began when they learned how to safeguard colonies found in the wild. By providing artificial shelters called hives, for swarms to settle in, people found that they could exercise some control

Plate 11-1. An Egyptian hieroglyph of a bee from an inscription dating from the New Kingdom 18th Dynasty. According to Egyptian mythology, bees were the tears of the sun god Ra. Bees were also the symbol of kingship not only in ancient Egypt, but also in central American Mayan culture. Karnak. Credit: Werner Forman/Universal Images Group/Getty Images. (see page 184)

Plate 11-2. (left) Dated at 6000 BC, this painting in the Cueva de la Araña (Spider Cave) in Valencia, Spain, illustrates the importance of honey for hunter-gatherers. Credit: Éric Tourneret. (right) Water-color painting copy of the original. Credit: Francisco Benítez Mellado/Fundación Provincial de Artes Plásticas Rafael Botí.

over the bees and their resources, honey and wax, could be exploited more easily. An early advance was the grouping together of hives to form an apiary, which enabled an individual or small community to produce a surplus of bee products which could be used in barter. Moreover, a honey surplus could be easily stored as a stand-by in times of food shortage.

In Egypt and China, bees have been kept in hives of one sort or another for at least 4,000 years. The species exploited by the Ancient Egyptians was the Western honeybee, *Apis mellifera*, which is native to Africa, Europe and the Middle East; another species, *A. cerana*, was used by the Chinese. The latter is restricted to roughly the monsoon lands of Asia, being found from Pakistan to Indonesia and north to Manchuria. Today, it is gradually being replaced by *A. mellifera* as a managed species. It is interesting to note that beekeeping arose independently in the West and in China, using two different species. (Plate 11-3)

Beekeeping is now big business, especially in the United States, Canada, Mexico and Australia. The average annual honey yield per hive is 50lb (22.68kg) in North America, while under the excellent conditions found in the Peace River region of Alberta, Canada, it can reach 300lb (136.08kg). An apiary may produce upwards of 100 tons (101.6 tonnes) per year and, on a world basis, the value of the honey crop in 1979 was about £20 million ($31.8 million). The value of agricultural crops dependent on the pollination services of bees is estimated at £1000 million ($1590 million) per annum, thus exceeding the value of honey produced by a factor of fifty.

Although our scientific knowledge of the honeybee is very detailed and beekeeping techniques are now very advanced, we cannot say that the honeybee is domesticated in the sense that, for example, the dog is domesticated. The behavior of dogs has been modified by thousands of years of selective breeding, so that they can get along with people and perform useful tasks; indeed, domestic animals are often trained to behave in ways which would be maladaptive in the wild. By using selective breeding, bee scientists have been able to modify certain behavioral traits in honeybee, such as improving relative docility and honey production.

Bees: A Natural History

Plate 11-3

Plate 11-3. The Western honeybee, *Apis mellifera*, left, is larger and the Oriental honeybee, *A. cerana*, right, is smaller and has more distinct bands. Credit: Paul Zbrowski/Queensland Government.

The honeybee, however, cannot be taught anything by beekeepers. The beekeeper uses his or her knowledge of bees to obtain honey and other products. So far as the bees are concerned, the colony might just as well be in a hollow tree trunk as in a modern hive. The basic repertoire of bee behavior remains as inviolate as it was before those Spanish cave paintings were conceived 9,000 years ago; man is still a robber of bees, albeit a sophisticated one.

For 90 percent of our history, we have been hunter-gatherers. Honey and bee grubs were and still are vital standby foods for such a lifestyle. This is exemplified with particular force by the Yanomamö Indians of the Venezuelan Brazilian borderlands. By the age of about eleven or twelve years, most individuals of this forest people can distinguish between twelve species of stingless bee, using a combination of

diagnostic characters which includes structure, of the bees themselves, their behavior and nest architecture. Professional entomologists require the aid of a microscope and specialized literature to accomplish the same feat.

The Kayapó Indians of the Amazonian provinces of Pára and Mato Grosso in Brazil are also accomplished taxonomists. They recognize 56 folk species of bee, 54 of which are stingless bees (*Trigona* and *Melipona* spp.). These folk species correspond to 66 species recognized by entomologists. The folk classification of the Kayapó therefore has an 86 percent correlation with the scientific classification. This is hardly surprising, for bees are important in the lives of these forest people. Their knowledge of the bees enables them to keep nine folk species in semi domestication.

A Murmur of Bees

The earliest references to beekeeping in Jewish writings are in the Talmud, the great Rabbinical text of religious observances, which evolved between 0 and 600 AD. It is interesting to note that honey is one of the few foods which are not considered unclean if left uncovered. (Plate 11-4)

Beekeeping has a long tradition in India and here, too, wild honey is highly prized. Professional honey gatherers collect honey from nests of the Giant Oriental honeybee, *Apis dorsata*. According to a report in 1980's, from the Indian Ministry of Forests, wild honey harvests declined by 50 percent because twenty nine honey collectors were eaten by tigers in the Calcutta area and their surviving colleagues had sought alternative employment.

By contrast, the honey hunters of Nepal are clearly willing to take considerable risks in practicing their livelihood: they gather honey from a close relative of the Giant Himalayan honeybee (*Apis laboriosa*). This bee produces a highly-prized commodity, "red" honey. It is so valuable that the honey hunters risk their lives on rickety rope ladders to gain access to nests high up on the cliff faces where they brave stings from the world's largest species of honeybee. (Plate 11-5)

The ownership of bee cliffs or access rights to them is an important indicator of personal wealth and

Plate 11-4. Archaeologists digging in Tel Rehov, northern Israel, have discovered evidence of an ancient beekeeping industry, including beehives made of mud and straw dated to around 900 BC. Credit: Amihai Mazar, The Hebrew University of Jerusalem.

until recently, was often an important component of marriage dowries. They do not sell the honey locally, but export it to Hong Kong, Japan and Korea, where its alleged relaxing and intoxicating properties are greatly valued.

Honey is regarded as so special that, even in societies in which the concept of personal property is alien, a wild honeybee colony is the only resource a person may regard as his or her own. It is a common practice to give a characteristic mark to the rock or hollow tree in which the colony lives. The community recognizes this sign of ownership, though typically, the produce of the colony is shared with everyone.

Honey was the most important sweetener in the west until the development of the sugar cane industry in the New World, which dates from the 15th century. The first alcoholic drinks were made from fermented honey.

In ancient Greece, there was a tradition of there being a time before wine made from grapes and honey drinks were the only intoxicating liquors. According to Plutarch, mead was used as a libation before wines were made. He writes: "Even now, those of the barbarians who do not drink wine have a honey drink." Mead was the commonest alcoholic drink in the middle Ages. During a time of severe drought in 1015, a fire broke out and threatened to engulf the German town of Meissen on the Upper Elbe; it was extinguished with mead, the most plentiful liquid ready to hand.

The antiquity of honey liquors can be gauged by the similarity of the words used to denote them; they all derive from the same root, dating from a time before the languages of the Indo European stem divided: *madhu* (Sanskrit), *methu* (Greek), *madu* (Avestan), *medus* (Lithuanian) and mead (Recent English).

Today, much of the honey produced in Africa is fermented and mixed with other substances to make a beer or mead for use in tribal rites. Among the Masai of East Africa, the ritual drinking of honey wine is important in circumcision ceremonies and can be drunk only by the elders. A married couple is always selected to brew the drink. The couple must remain chaste for two days before brewing starts and for the six days of its duration. The belief is that the wine will

be undrinkable and that the bees will abscond if the couple fails to observe the rule.

Honey is not the only bee product used by man. Wax has been used for thousands of years in candles, and today the Catholic Church only uses candles made from beeswax for liturgical use.

Beeswax is also used in the casting of metal objects. The "lost wax" method of casting metal ornaments and statues was developed independently by several cultures. This entails the sculpting in beeswax of a model, complete with all the fine detail required in the finished product. The model is then covered with layers of fine clay, with passages to allow molten metal to be poured in. A final layer of coarse clay is applied and the model is then heated so that wax

Bees: A Natural History

Plate 11-5

melts and runs away through an aperture. Molten metal is poured into the mould and when it has cooled, the clay is broken away to reveal a metal replica of the original wax model.

The "lost wax" method of casting in metal was developed in South America by the Chibcha of Columbia, using the wax of stingless bees, *Melipona* spp. and *Trigona* spp. and craftsmen in peninsular India use the wax of the Giant Oriental honeybee, *Apis dorsata*; the Chinese have used the wax of the Lesser Oriental honeybee, *A. cerana* from about 2,500 BC. The most famous exponents of the "lost wax method", however, are the metal smiths of the Benin culture in Nigeria. They have used the wax of the Western honeybee *A. mellifera* since about 1300 AD and today,

Benin City is still the home of fine craftsmen working in bronze.

Modern jewellery designers also use wax from *A. mellifera* and the newest use of this 6000 year old craft tradition is in the casting of turbine blades for the engines of jet aircraft.

Plate 11-5. In order to gain access to the inner, honey-bearing comb, of the Giant Himalayan honeybee, *Apis laboriosa*, these Nepalese honey hunters must first slice away the outer comb occupied by brood cells. They use a long bamboo pole fitted with a wooden tip whittled to form a flat blade. Credit: Éric Tourneret.

Plate 12–1

Bees in Folklore

12

Although the honeybee has played an important part in human economy from the very beginnings of civilization, it was only in the latter half of the eighteenth century that honeybees were shown to mate, in flight, away from the hive. Until then, it was thought that the species was devoid of sexuality and so chastity was one of the many virtues attributed to it. This created a problem: if bees did not mate like other animals, then it became necessary to explain their continued presence and multiplication. Folklore is therefore rich in theories of bee genesis.

The Greeks and Romans believed that bees sucked their young fully formed out of flowers. This was perpetuated in Virgil's fourth book of Georgics, which is largely devoted to bees. He wrote:

> "...they [the bees] neither rejoice in bodily union,
> nor waste themselves in love's langours nor bring
> forth their young by pain of birth; but alone from
> the leaves of sweet scented herbage, they gather
> their children in their mouths, thus sustaining their
> strength of tiny citizens."

Another legend from classical times attributes the creation of bees to the god Jupiter. As an infant, he was entrusted by his mother, Ops, to Melissa and Amalthea, the beautiful daughters of the King of Crete, to save them from his father, Saturn, who was in the habit of eating his own offspring. When Jupiter was old enough to take his place with the other gods, he expressed his gratitude to Melissa by turning her into a bee with the ability to reproduce herself without mating. Amalthea's reward was to be placed in the sky as the star Capella. More recently, Amalthea was memorialized by the 19th century French entomologist, Olivier, who named a stingless bee after her, *Trigona amalthea*.

In Brittany, devout Christians believed for generations that bees were created from tears shed by Christ as he hung on the cross. Each tear turned into a bee which flew off to become a provider of sweetness for humankind. It is surprising that this belief persisted for so long, for the person well versed in the Bible would surely have known that bees pre dated the Crucifixion. How else could Israel have been described in the Old Testament as flowing with milk and honey? Had the good folk of Brittany consulted the Book of Judges, they would have found a reference to the age old belief that bees were generated from the bodies of dead lions. When that most ardent of biblical lovers, Samson, went a wooing to Timnah, he killed a young lion in the vineyards there. On his way home, he found a swarm of bees, complete with honey, in the lion's carcass. This prompted his famous riddle:

"Out of the eater came forth meat and out of the strong came forth sweetness."
Judges 14:14

The belief that bees originate from the corpses of noble animals such as the lion is thought to have originated in Egypt. It was taken up by the Greeks and Romans, though they substituted the corpses of oxen for those of lions. Virgil gives a detailed description:

> *"Next is found a two year old bull calf, whose crooked*
> *horns bee just beginning to bud; the beast, his nose*
> *holes and breathing are stopped, in spite of his much*
> *kicking; and after he hath been thumped to death, his*
> *entrails, bruised as they bee, melt inside his entire skin.*
> *This done, he is left in the place afore prepared, and*
> *under his sides are put bitts of boughes, and thyme, and*
> *fresh plucked rosemariae. And all this doethe take place*
> *at the season when the zephyrs are first curling the*
> *waters, before the meades be ruddy with their spring tide*
> *colours, and before the swallow, that leetle chatterer,*
> *doethe hang her nest again the beam. In time, the*

Plate 12–1. The Indian bee goddess, Bhramari Devi. (see page 194)

Bees: A Natural History

warm humour beginneth to ferment inside the soft
bones of the carcass; and wonderfull to tell, there
appear creatures, footless at first, but which soon getting
unto themselves winges, mingle together and buzz
about, joying more and more in their airy life. At last,
burst they forth, thick as rain droppes from a summer cloude,
thick as arrowes, the which leave the clanging stringes
when the nimble Parthians make their battles onsett."
Fourth Book of Georgics
(Old, anonymous translation)

The "footless creatures" were, of course, the maggots or larvae of carrion flies such as the blowflies *Calliphora* spp. or fleshflies, *Lucilia* spp. To the unaided eye they would have appeared very similar to the larvae of bees. Likewise, the buzzing of the adult flies would have resembled that of bees.

In Athens, at the time of Pericles, there were said to be 20,000 hives and we must remember that the ancients had none of the modern means of swarm prevention. Moreover, their simple, unsophisticated hives would have meant that the absconding of colonies would be much more prevalent than it is today. Thus, if the ox rite was carried out in a beekeeping area at the right time of year, there would be a good chance that a swarm would settle in the vicinity and belief in the rite would be vindicated. If the rite failed, there were many gods of a malevolent nature who could take the blame.

Virgil's fourth book of Georgics is a work of great lyrical charm. It is also a guide to practical beekeeping in which hard facts and keen observation abide side by side with fanciful notions such as the generation of bees from putrid flesh. Nevertheless, it was the basis of most beekeeping manuals until the eighteenth and nineteenth centuries. Even the ox rite claimed adherents. In the early 1800's, a Mr. Carew, of Anthony, Cornwall, claimed to have followed Virgil's directions with complete success.

In classical literature, one is likely to encounter perfectly accurate descriptions of bee behavior but with absurd interpretations. Plutarch, for example, thought that some bees carried small stones as ballast when flying in blustery weather. In 100 BC, he wrote:

"The bees of Candi, being about to double a point or
cape lying into the sea, which is much exposed to the
winds, they ballast themselves with small grit or
petty stones, for to be able to endure the weather and
not be carried away against their wills with the winds
through their lightness otherwise."

About 100 years later, Virgil referred to this:

"And as when empty barks on billows float,
With sandy ballast sailors trim the boat,
So bees bear gravel stones whose poising weight,
Steers through the whistling winds their steady flight."
Georgics IV
(Translated by John Dryden)

There is no doubt about the accuracy of the observation. Bees are often seen carrying small stones or pellets of mud between their jaws. The bees, however, are not honeybees, but solitary mason bees (see Chapter 3); they carry these loads not for ballast but for nest construction. Such bees are especially common in the Mediterranean region, where Plutarch and Virgil lived.

Many old beliefs about honeybees are concerned with swarms; the time of year when they occur and where they alight. The Greeks believed that if a swarm landed on the mouth of an infant, then he was destined to be eloquent in adult life. Plato, Sophocles and Xenophon were all thought to have benefited from such a visitation and it appears that all three shared the nickname "Bee of Attica" or "The Athenian Bee."

The Greeks also believed that the swarming of a colony heralded the arrival of a stranger; the Romans feared it as an ill omen. The famous general, Scipio, it is reported, refused to advance during one military campaign because a swarm of honeybees had alighted in his camp. The death of the Emperor Claudius was predicted by a swarm which landed in his tent and, when a swarm settled on the Capitol in Rome, the citizens were greatly disturbed.

A belief in the dreadful implications of a swarm was widespread and persisted until quite recent times. In Ireland, a swarm meant an imminent death in the family of the beekeeper. In both Norfolk and Switzerland, death in the family was certain if the swarm settled on rotten wood.

In some societies, people believed that a swarm, far from being a harbinger of doom, was a sure sign of good luck. Austrian beekeepers believed that a person's prosperity was assured if a swarm alighted on the house. It is said that in Poland, when the throne was vacant, a man was chosen to be king because a swarm had landed on him and this ensured a long and peaceful reign.

In parts of Germany, it was once believed lucky to possess a branch on which a swarm had clustered. People went to much trouble to extract the maximum benefit from such a talisman. For example, if a farmer made a cross out of such a branch on Good Friday and used it to drive his cattle to market, then he was assured of a good price for his stock.

Traditionally, a swarm has always ceased to be the property of a beekeeper if it leaves his land and if he does not seek actively to recover it. Thus, irrespective of whether swarming was regarded as a sign of good or bad luck, it was still necessary to try to get the swarm into a hive as soon as possible. This gave rise to many quaint customs. Virgil and Pliny recommended the banging of pans and the ringing of bells to make a swarm settle. This was later modified to become a public warning to the neighbors that a hive had swarmed.

Many charms and spells were used to induce swarms to settle:

"Christ, the swarm is out! Now my beasts, fly here, into the peace of the Lord, into the protection of God, to come home safe. Sit, sit bees: Holy Mary commanded you. May you have no leave to go, may you fly not to the wood, you will neither escape from me nor break away from me. Sit very still, do God's will."

Another spell, from eleventh century Germany involved throwing sand over the swarm and reciting:

**"Settle, victorious women, sink down to earth.
You must never fly wild to the wood.
Be as mindful of my welfare
As every man is of food and home."**
From ninth century Old High German

The reference to worker bees as "women'" is interesting, for it is the earliest example I know of an intuitive understanding of the sex of worker honeybees.

For English beekeepers, it was once the custom to stand by a hive which threatened to swarm and sing songs. If the bees were kept amused, it was thought, they would be reluctant to go.

Beekeeping is widespread in Africa and the hiving of a swarm is usually attended by ritual observances. When, for example, a Bantu man in South Africa starts beekeeping for the first time, he is never allowed to stock his first hive himself. Instead, an uncle must do it for him, and the budding beekeeper must abstain from marital relations until the colony is established. Cohabitation can be resumed only after the swarm has been in the hive for two days and the workers have started to build new comb.

Clearly, the earlier a swarm is hived and the colony begins to store honey, the greater will be the yield for the beekeeper. This fact gave rise to a verse which, in various forms, is found in much of Europe:

*" A swarm in May is worth a load of hay,
A swarm in June is worth a silver spoon,
A swarm in July is not worth a fly."*

In the early days of American beekeeping, the Rev. Thomas P. Hunt invented a strange device which, he claimed, would induce a swarm to settle and cluster, so that the beekeeper could gather it and place it in a hive. Hunt called his device a "bee-bob" and it consisted of enough dead honeybee workers strung together by needle and thread to form a ball the size of an egg. It was necessary to have some loose threads, with bees attached, extending out from the ball. The bee bob was attached to the end of a pole, which was waved about in the apiary. The theory was that the ball suggested a swarm cluster and persuaded swarming bees to settle. The Rev. Hunt claimed that his method was infallible. (Plate 12-2)

We saw in Chapter 4 that when scout bees have found a suitable nesting site, they emit an attractive scent from the Nasonov glands in their abdomens; more and more workers are thus recruited and eventually, the swarm moves to the new nest site. Although the Rev. Hunt could not have known of the existence or function of the Nasonov gland scent, he might have unwillingly put it to use: if he had used freshly killed bees in his bee bob, then there was a good chance that the abdomens of some of them would have been damaged and scent released from the Nasonov glands, with the desired result.

In 1975, an American researcher, J.T. Ambrose, showed that there may be a rational basis for Hunt's method. He found that if balls of soft beeswax were impregnated with scents extracted from the Nasonov glands of worker honeybees, they were invariably attractive to swarms. In eight experiments conducted with his latter day bee bob, Ambrose had complete success in attracting swarms.

Until recently, so much of what went on in the hive was a mystery. If the colony was able to conduct its affairs with such orderly co-operation and construct wax combs of such regular beauty, then it was held to be a self evident truth that bees were very wise.

Thus, beekeepers have always regarded their bees with awe and respect and many supernatural abilities were attributed to them. They could predict rain and were skilled astronomers. Naturally, they were devout

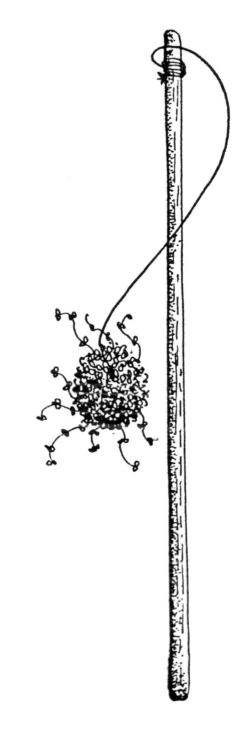

Plate 12-2. The Rev. Thomas P. Hunt's "bee-bob" a device supposed to induce a honeybee swarm to settle in a convenient spot for ease of capture by the beekeeper. Credit: Christopher O'Toole.

"Went drearily singing the chore-girl small."

Bees: A Natural History

and at midnight on Christmas Eve they always hummed hymns to celebrate the birth of Christ. When a colony was not doing well, it was often thought to be in need of spiritual sustenance and Bedfordshire beekeepers would stand in front of the hive and sing psalms.

There used to be widespread belief in Europe that bees could detect profanity and vice in people. Immorality on the part of the beekeeper would drive his bees into a fury and he would be stung. Young women would test the moral soundness of their suitors by leading them through an apiary and noting the bees' response.

Central European beekeepers took their relationship with bees so seriously that they used to give the bees written contracts, guaranteeing good care and management throughout the year.

"Telling the bees" is an old custom which is widespread in Europe and one which was taken by early settlers to North America. It is believed that the relationship of the beekeeper with his bees is so close that they must be told if the beekeeper has died; otherwise, the bees themselves would decline and die. In England, France and Germany, the bees were told by a member of the bereaved family who would knock on the hive three times, saying "The Master is dead. The Master is dead."

In Guernsey, one of the British Channel Islands, the relation would knock on the hive with the key to the house. If the bees replied with a hum, it was understood that they agreed to stay and provide the new owner with honey. The mourners then decked out the hives with black crepe, or placed a small piece of black wood on top of each one and the apiary entered a period of mourning for six months. Some of the cake and wine which was served to the mourners was placed in each hive.

"Telling the Bees" was the subject of a poem by the American writer John Greenleaf Whittier (1807–92). The poem describes how a beemaster, on returning home after a long absence, finds one of the serving girls telling the bees of the death of someone. As he listens, the awful realization dawns on him that it is his wife who has died:

Before them, under the garden wall,
Forward and back,
Went drearily singing the chore girl small,
Draping each hive with a shred of black.
Trembling, I listened: the summer sun
Had the chill of snow;
For I knew she was telling the bees of one
Gone on the journey we all must go!

The I said to myself, 'My Mary weeps
For the dead today:
Haply her blind old grandsire sleeps
The threat and pain of his age away'.

But her dog whined low; on the doorway sill,
With his cane to his chin,
The old man sat; and the chore girl still
Sung to the bees stealing out and in.

And the song she was singing ever since
In my ear sounds on:
'Stay at home pretty bees, fly not hence!
Mistress Mary is dead and gone!'

It was not only in times of grief that bees were invited to join in family affairs. If there was a wedding, the bees were invited to the celebrations and the hives were suitably decorated. In Brittany, they were clothed with red cloth and, in Northamptonshire, it was the custom to place a piece of the wedding cake in each hive.

Throughout England, the bees were told not only about family matters but also events of public concern. They would be notified of the birth of a royal heir or the declaration of war.

One of the commonest themes in bee lore is the desire of royalty to be associated in some way with bees. Indeed, the queen bee was once regarded as the king of the colony. The image of a monarch surrounded by thousands of totally loyal, obedient worker subjects was irresistible.

The earliest record of a link between bees and royalty comes from Egypt. Ancient hieroglyphics are rich in references to bees and beekeeping. From about 3,500 BC until Roman times, the hieroglyphic symbol for the king was a bee.

In Europe, bees were used in the burial rites of the Frankish kings. When Childéric I died, 300 gold bees were placed in the tomb where he was buried, although some authorities think that the little gold effigies in fact depicted cicadas. (Plate 12-3)

Napoleon Bonaparte was fascinated by the order and industry of the hive and selected images of bees for his coat of arms; his green coronation robe was decorated with a golden bee motif. (Plate 12-4) An analogy between the bee kingdom and that of man is drawn by the Archbishop of Canterbury in Shakespeare's Henry V, Act 1, Scene ii:

> *So work the honeybees,*
> *Creatures that by a rule in nature teach*
> *The art of order to a peopled kingdom;*
> *They have a king and officers of sorts;*
> *Where some like magistrates, remain at home,*
> *Others, like merchants venture trade abroad;*
> *Others like soldiers armed in their stings,*
> *Make boot upon the summer's velvet buds;*
> *Which pillage they with merry march bring home*
> *To the royal tent of their emperor;*
> *Who, buried in his majesty, surveys*
> *The singing masons building roofs of gold,*
> *The civil citizens kneading up the honey,*
> *The poor mechanic porters crowding in*
> *Their heavy burdens at his narrow gate,*
> *The sad eyed justice with his surly hum,*
> *Delivering o'er to executor pale*
> *The lazy yawning drones.*

If the ordered society of the hive was an inspiration to monarchs and militarists, it was an equally important source of inspiration for religions. A whole chapter of the Koran is devoted to the honeybee. Muslims believe it to be the only animal with which Allah regularly converses and it is the only animal to go to heaven when it dies. Both the Muslim and Christian faiths shared the belief that bees were the only animals which remained unchanged when they left Paradise. Beeswax was, therefore, an appropriate substance from which to make church candles and to this day the Roman Catholic Church insists on pure beeswax candles for liturgical use.

For centuries, the honeybee and its alleged virtues exercised a powerful hold on the imaginations of moralists and theologians. This reached its zenith in the eighteenth and nineteenth centuries, when many books and pamphlets were published. Several were written by country parsons and even books on the purely practical aspects of beekeeping invariably had a sermonizing preface or introduction. One such book, published in 1743 and written by an Oxfordshire rector, the Rev. John Thorley, opens with a bombastic attack on the moral turpitude of the day. He writes, addressing the 'Candid and Judicious Reader':

> *"In an age of reigning infidelity, when vice and*
> *immorality are under no restraint, but practised*
> *with impunity, and without control, triumphing over*
> *all laws, both human and divine; when men not*
> *only degrade and vilify the sacred oracles; look on*
> *the Gospel as no better than a cunningly devised*
> *fable, and the most important truths, as the greatest*
> *impertinencies; and treat the blessed author*
> *of our most holy religion as a vile and wicked*
> *imposter; but also dispute and even deny the being*
> *of a God; a serious essay to establish the first*
> *principle of religion..."*

> *Melissologia or the Female Monarchy*

This goes on for nine pages, leading up to his final point, which he brandishes like the proof of a geometric theorem. We can summarize it as follows: The splendors of Nature and her intricate workings testify to the existence of a Supreme Being, a Creator. Next to humankind, the honeybee is the finest work of God

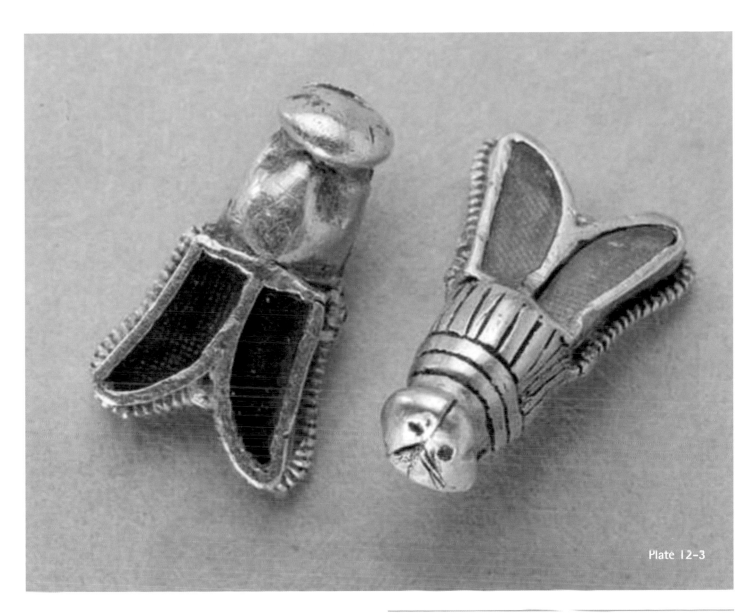

Plate 12-3. In 1653 a mason working on the reconstruction of the church of Saint Brice in Tournai discovered a forgotten Merovingian tomb. The tomb contained a leather purse of gold and silver coins, a richly ornamented sword as well as other weapons, various items of jewelry fashioned from gold and cloisonnéed garnet, a golden bull's head, an ornate harness studded with gold flowers, and 300 golden bees. Among these artifacts was a ring inscribed with the words CHILDERICI REGIS, which led to the tomb being identified as that of Childéric I (ca. 426–481). Credit: Bibliothèque nationale de France.

Plate 12-4

and it follows that the husbandry of bees contributes to the economic vitality of the nation, and is, moreover, spiritually wholesome in that it confronts man with living proof of the existence of God. Also, the bees' virtues, chastity, temperance, industry and maternal devotion, are a lesson to believers and unbelievers alike. After this, Thorley calms down and there follows a sedate, anecdotal account of beekeeping in eighteenth century England.

Exactly 100 years later, another Oxfordshire cleric, the Rev. William C. Cotton, sometime student of Christ Church and founder member of the Oxford Apiarian Society, sought to promote beekeeping as an answer to the moral, social and economic ills of the rural poor. To this end he published two pamphlets, one called *A Short and Simple Letter to Cottagers from a Bee Preserver* and another called *Letters to Cottagers on the Natural Theology of Bees*. These were written in a style which today would be regarded as patronizing and offensive. In *My Bee Book*, a collected edition of his writings, published in 1842 with the gentry in mind, he describes his prose as being deliberately simple because of the proverbial stupidity of the English peasant.

Cotton's proselytizing zeal for beekeeping was not reserved for the lowly poor. One of the aims of the Oxford Apiarian Society was 'to promote a more extensive knowledge concerning the natural history and cultivation of bees among the higher classes'. His hope was that the gentry would spread the good word to the poor. In the preface to *My Bee Book*, Cotton wrote:

> "...a row of Bees keeps a man at home; all his spare moments may be well filled by tending them, by watching their wondrous ways, and by loving them. In winter, he may work in his own chimney corner, at making Hives both for himself and to sell. This he will find almost as profitable as his Bees, for well made Hives always meet a ready sale. Again, his Beehives are close to his cottage door; he will learn to like their sweet music better than the dry squeaking of the pot house fiddle, and he may listen to it in the free open air, with his wife and children about him. This will be to him a countless family, he will be sure to love them if he cares for them, and they will love him too, and repay all his pains. Many a lesson a man and his wife may teach their children at the mouth of their Hives; for a Bee garden is only second to a Sunday school."
>
> (pp. xliii xliv)

Cotton then goes on to exploit the old belief, referred to earlier, that bees express their disapproval of immorality by producing poor honey yields. He does not seem to have considered a simpler explanation, namely that drunkards and lechers were hardly likely to take good care of their bees. He writes, sternly:

> " A good Bee master must not be unchaste and uncleanly; for impurity and sluttiness (themselves being most chaste and neat) they utterly abhor; you must not come among them smelling of sweat, or having a stinking breath, caused either through eating of leaks, onion, garlic and the like, or by any other means, the noisomeness where whereof is corrected with a cup of beer; you must not be given to surfeiting or drunkenness."
>
> (p. xliv)

Plate 12-4. At his coronation on December 2, 1804, Napoleon Bonaparte wore a crimson robe decorated with embroidered gold bees based on those found in Childéric's tomb. Napoleon chose the bee as a symbol of his new empire in order to link his reign to that of Childéric, the first king of France. Bees symbolized immortality and resurrection, and were considered the oldest emblem of French sovereignty. The bees replaced the *fleur-de-lis* of the old regime and appear on imperial tapestries and garments, as well as on Napoleonic era clothing, carpets, and furniture all across France. *Napoléon Ier en costume de sacre* by Robert Lefebvre (1811). Credit: Musée national de la Légion d'honneur et des ordres de chevalerie, Paris.

Here, Cotton places himself in a dilemma, because, while extolling the temperance of bees, he has to contend with two awkward facts. First, a common winter food provided for bees at that time, and one which he recommends himself, was a mixture of beer and sugar. Second, he suggests that, because bees can be irritated by human breath, beekeepers should sweeten it with beer, especially after eating garlic and onions. The British art of compromise wins through, however. Cotton allows that the beekeeper may drink beer without undermining his aspirations to temperance so long as it is drunk solely for the purpose of sweetening the breath for the sake of the bees. Presumably, it was actually bad form to enjoy the beer.

Logical consistency, however, did not deter these exponents of hive theology. There were no lengths to which the fanatical Cotton would not go to promote beekeeping. He even rewrote Coleridge's great epic poem, *The Rime of the Ancient Mariner*, to include beekeeping references which were not in the original. For example, Coleridge wrote:

**"Farewell, farewell! but this I tell
To thee thou Wedding Guest!
He prayeth well who loveth well
Both man and bird and beast."**
Part the Seventh, stanza 22

Cotton altered this to:

"Farewell, farewell but this I tell
To thee, Bee master blest,
He playeth best who loveth best
Both man and bird and beast."
My Bee Book p. 20

After this quotation, Cotton admits to making modifications "for the purpose." One feels he would have had no qualms about rewriting the Bible if it were not already so rich in allusions to bees.

While it is easy to scorn the peculiar zeal of clerical writers such as Thorley and Cotton, it should be remembered that they did much, through their books, to improve the efficiency of beekeeping practices among rural folk.

Not all cultures regard bees as exemplars of moral behaviour, though. In the plains of India, several large, dark species of carpenter bee (*Xylocopa* spp.) are held in affection: in romantic Sanskrit poetry, these bees, *bhramara* or *bhowra*, symbolize either lovers or, sometimes, loose morals. (see Plate 12-1)

The criminal fraternity in India had a more practical use for these bees. Thieves would trap the bees in a box until nightfall and then release the bhramara *karandaka*, which flew into the candles or lamps of the houses to be robbed, plunging the victims into darkness and confusion.

The honeybee has a special place in the Mormon religion. The Book of Mormon, published in 1830, tells how the honeybee, called *deseret*, was carried by the Jaredites into the valley of Nimrod. The word *deseret* has mystical significance for Mormons and when Utah was admitted to the Union in 1896, Deseret was the first name proposed for the state. Today, the state seal features a beehive surrounded by flowers and the motto "Industry." (Plate 12-5) In the United States, Utah is known colloquially as the "Beehive State."

Despite this, the honeybee is not native to North America and it is thought to have been first introduced into New England by settlers in 1638. It has even been suggested that honeybees might have been introduced by Irish or Viking voyagers between 800 and 900 AD.

Native Americans quickly learned how to rob the wild colonies which had escaped as swarms from the hives of European settlers. By 1706, the Cherokee themselves had learned to keep bees in hollow log hives and had a flourishing trade in honey and wax. It is intriguing to note that although beekeeping was so recent a development in Cherokee culture, they have no tradition of there being "a time before honeybees."

The honeybee was not introduced into South America until the nineteenth century. Nevertheless, the Spanish conquistadors were offered gifts of honey and they recorded that tributes of honey and beeswax were paid to the Inca ruler Tup Yupanqui. The honey and beeswax were gathered from the native stingless bees, the nests being found in hollow trees and rock crevices. (see Chapter 2).

Plate 12-5. The old fashioned "skep" hive is featured on the state seal of Utah as well as on road signs within the state.

Two species, the Mayan Stingless bee, *Melipona beechei*, another stingless bee, *Trigona cupira*, are still kept in hollow log hives by the people of Yucatan.

Earlier, in the fifteenth century, honey was one of the gifts given to Columbus by the aboriginal people of Cuba, the Taino and Ciboney. There is no doubt that the Pre Columbians carried swarms or nests of Mayan Stingless bees from Central America to Cuba, Jamaica and possibly Hispaniola, long before the arrival of Europeans.

The Maya in Central America and the later Aztec civilization in Mexico, had systems of hieroglyphic writing in which stingless bees and their nests were portrayed. (Plate 12-6) Some of the manuscripts have been preserved and are known as the American Codices.

It is interesting to note that bees and honey were important in three of the great dynastic civilizations, the Ancient Egyptians, the Mayas and the Aztecs. All three cultures venerated the bee, associated bees with kingship or deity and later came to imbue honey with the power to increase longevity. The hieroglyphics of the three cultures are rich in references to bee husbandry. Mayan populations in the Northern Petén region of what is now Guatemala venerated a god called Aprime and his image is preserved in buried clay vessels used as hives for stingless bees. (Plate 12-5).

This pre-occupation with bees is an example of cultural convergence, for the Ancient Egyptians and South American civilizations were totally isolated from each other, yet developed very similar beliefs about different bees, the Western honeybee, *Apis mellifera* and the stingless bees *Melipona* spp. and *Trigona* spp.

Given the long association between people and bees, it is inevitable that honey and other bee products would be imbued with as many magical and mystical properties as were the bees themselves. Wherever honey was gathered, whether from wild colonies or from managed hives, it was used as a libation to deities and as a gift of appeasement to devils and demons; the Greeks regarded honey as the food of the gods.

There was and still is a close physical relationship between beekeepers and their bees. In Central and Eastern Europe hives are often incorporated into the sides of

Plate 12-6. A painted clay vessel of a type used in Mayan as hives for stingless bees. The figure is that of the God Aprime, indicated by marks on his cheeks and thighs. He was the patron of beekeepers and, under the name Ah Kan, also the god of wine (fermented honey drink). Loosely translated, the text over his head reads in part loose "he grabs or catches, he gathers sweet." This type of vessel has been used as bee hives in Yucatan even in modern times. Credit: Justin Kerr/The Maya Vase Database.

houses or may be sited in elaborately decorated "bee houses." This physical closeness meant that the bees were just as susceptible as their master or mistress to bad spells and the evil eye. It was just as vital, therefore, to protect the hives as it was to protect the house.

In the Middle East, beekeepers ensured the good fortune of their bees by burying the eye of a bear or the liver of a White falcon beneath the hive. Even today, in the Caucasus, beekeepers ward off the evil eye by placing the skull of a horse or cow on top of each hive.

The latter practice was widespread in Europe until quite recently and I witnessed something like it in northwest Spain in 1967. On the southern slopes of the Sierra del Eje, I came across a village where beekeeping seemed to be the main livelihood. The hillsides were littered with cylindrical hives made from the bark of cork oaks; the roof of each hive was a piece of slate and the hives stood on the steep slopes, looking like the gaunt statues of Easter Island.

It was high summer and the vegetation on the hills was burnt up, brown and dead looking in the strong sun. As I rested in some shade, I saw a group of ten or fifteen people toiling up the road in my direction. They stopped near a group of hives just below me. Two or three men of the party went among the hives, looking inside a few, listening to others. When this inspection was over, they returned to their companions on the road and watched, as a girl of perhaps eighteen years, went down among the hives.

She carried a basket containing what looked like white stones or bleached bones, pieces of which she placed on the roof of each hive. As she moved between the hives, she started to sing. Her wordless song echoed across the valleys and hills. She was singing to the bees. And the sound of her voice was grave and beautiful in the distance.

Plate 13-1

Bees in Folk and Modern Medicine

13

Adult bees have at various times been used in folk medicine. In Europe, the ashes derived from burnt honeybees were once used as a cure for baldness. The Lao people of Cambodia treat sore throats in children with a mixture of milk and pounded up, roasted adults of the carpenter bee, *Xylocopa aestuans*. This species, called *Mang poo* in Lao, is also eaten.

Most frequently, however, it is bee products rather then the bees themselves which have played an important role in folk medicine. Shamans of the Mnong Gar, a tribe of Montagnard people from the central highlands of Vietnam, use the resin nests of solitary mason bees, *khaang,* in the treatment of malarial fever. They burn the resin, together with powdered rice and saffron, to produce a thick, acrid smoke, which the patient inhales.

The earliest written medical prescription which survives is also the earliest known reference to honey. It consists of a stone tablet bearing Sumerian script, found at Nippur in Iraq. The tablet dates from 2100–2000 BC and gives directions for the preparation of an ointment, which contains honey, river sediments and cedar oil.

Honey is very popular with health food enthusiasts and practitioners of herbal medicine. Honeybees have an important place in the iconography of health food advertising copy. Even in advertisements for foods containing no honey or other bee products, a beehive in a pastoral setting is often depicted in the background, symbolizing "naturalness," "purity" and, no doubt, dietry virtue.

Exponents of naturopathy claim that honey contains "vital life forces." As recently as 1974, Henry Rowsell, master carpenter and part time amateur gynecologist, attributed mystical powers to honey.

In the introduction to his book *Henry's Bee Herbal: Modern Applications of Honey Therapy*, he quotes a statement of anthroposophist philosophy which sets the tone for the rest of the book. Honeybees store honey in hexagonal cells because this is a reflection of the fact that the natural crystal structure of quartz is hexagonal; plants absorb quartz from the soil; the quartz finds its way into the nectar which bees collect and convert into honey. Honey, therefore contains the formative force of quartz, which induces them to construct hexagonal cells. Humans need this formative force if their blood is to function properly. Honey, therefore, is a vital food.

This is a convoluted form of the medieval Doctrine of Signatures. Adherents of this doctrine held that God, in His infinite mercy and wisdom, laid his 'signature' on herbs of medicinal value, to indicate which ailment a particular herb was suitable for. Thus, those species of liverworts which grow as a flattened, flattened leafless thallus, with their liver shaped lobes, cured liver disorders; eyebright, with its eye like markings, relieved problems with the eyes. Notions of this kind persist today in the common belief that fish is good for the brain because it is supposed to resemble brain tissue and that tomatoes are good for the blood because they are red.

More than 180 substances have been identified in honey, but the formative force is not one of them; it remains as elusive as the unicorn.

Plate 13-1. A hairy arm is no defense against this stinging worker honeybee. Backwardly-directed barbs on her sting snag in the flesh, and her struggles to free herself mean the sting remains behind, with the muscular venom sac continuing to inject venom and she soon dies. Research has shown that some components of bee venom may have a role in the treatment of arthritis. Credit: Edward Ross. (see page 210)

Honey does, however, have practical and genuine uses in medicine. It has long been used for the relief of coughs and sore throats. It is also very useful in the sobering up of very drunk patients. Fructose, one of its main constituents, is absorbed very rapidly and helps to detoxify the alcohol in the bloodstream and liver.

The preservative properties of honey have been well known since the time of the Ancient Egyptians, who used honey extensively in the preparation of mummies. There is a story that some tomb robbers in Egypt came across a jar containing honey and began to eat it. One of the men found a hair on the hand he had been dipping into the honey. They then found that the jar contained the body of a small child, perfectly preserved and very well dressed. This story may be apocryphal, but perfectly edible honey, at least 3,000 years old, has been found in Egyptian tombs.

The preservative properties of honey lie in its composition. Ripe honey is a concentrated mixture of fructose, glucose, and small amounts of other sugars. There are traces of vitamins, minerals, gums and enzymes.

Research in India showed that honey may have a part to play in transplant surgery. Aortic valves were preserved in honey at 4°C (39°F); when reconstituted in saline solution, they regained their normal size, shape and texture. Unexpectedly, their tensile strength had increased by 50 percent.

Strong sugar concentrates such as honey are hygroscopic. This means that they have a great affinity for water, a property that is easy to demonstrate. If a jar of honey is left without its lid, it will become watery because the honey absorbs moisture from the air. This is why honeybees cap their storage cells with wax as soon as they have ripened the honey.

The combination of hygroscopic properties with traces of naturally occurring hydrogen peroxide makes honey a powerful, bactericide. Bacteria are killed by simple dehydration; the honey absorbs the moisture on which they depend. Thus, the time honored use of honey in the treatment of wounds has a rational basis and cannot be dismissed as an old wives' tale.

There have been several articles in the recent medical literature describing the use of honey in the treatment of burns and in the post operative care of patients with large surgical wounds. It appears that the honey dries the wound; in one study, bacteria cultured from surgical wounds were killed by undiluted honey.

Honey has several advantages over antibiotic drip feeds or dressings impregnated with antibiotics: it is an effective bactericide without being toxic to the patient and is also soluble in water. Moreover, it is most unlikely that bacteria will ever develop resistance to the devastating effects of desiccation. Honey is also cheap and easily available and, therefore, presumably of no interest to the drug companies. Why use inexpensive and safe substances like honey, when it is so easy to persuade the medical profession to use expensive ones?

Experiments with boar semen stored in dilute honey showed that the sugars protected the

Plate 13-2

214 Bees: A Natural History

spermatozoa from the effects of freezing and the small amounts of vitamins sustained the sperm for longer after thawing than conventional methods. Honey may therefore play a useful role in artificial insemination by donor routines and in vitro fertilization programs.

Many claims have been made about the aphrodisiac properties of honey. While bearing in mind that aphrodisiacs are mostly only effective in the minds of believers, there may nevertheless be something in these claims. The sugars in honey are rapidly absorbed into the bloodstream and if sexual powers are flagging because of simple fatigue, then honey may indeed help.

The Phoenicians believed that the alleged longevity of the Ancient Britons derived from the large amounts of honey and mead they consumed. The belief that honey improves longevity is common and persists among many peoples. During the Soviet period in Russia, gerontology, the study of aging processes, was taken very seriously. There were twelve major medical centers devoted to the specialty, all charged with increasing the productive lifespan of the workers. Russian gerontologists have studied the life styles of societies noted for their longevity. Paying particular attention to long lived people in Georgia, they found that beehive scrap is commonly eaten. This is a viscous mixture of honey, pollen and dead bees found at the bottom of hives.

The Russians concluded that the large amount of pollen in beehive scrap had revitalizing properties. Pollen, they found, contained fourteen vitamins, eleven minerals, eleven enzymes, seven pigments, sixteen fatty acids, six carbohydrates, nineteen amino acids,

Plate 13-2. A worker honeybee adds royal jelly to a queen cell. This substance is essential for colony development and is secreted by the pharyngeal glands of nurse bees and, mixed with pre-digested pollen, is an exceptional nutrient: it allows bee larvae to grow at a pace with no equivalent in the rest of the animal kingdom. Credit: Éric Tourneret.

oils, traces of about twelve other substances and a mysterious 3 percent which eluded analysis.

Quite independently of the Russians, a British food scientist, Neill Lyall, famed inventor of the meatless sausage, had come to the same conclusion. He noted that beehive scrap was common to the diets of long lived peoples in South America, Pakistan and Russia. Lyall now markets pollen in tablet form, claiming that it brings relief to sufferers with arthritis and stimulates the pancreas of the diabetic to produce more insulin. Pollen tablets are said also to relieve depression, piles, fatigue and the common cold. Inevitably, pollen is now claimed to be a powerful aphrodisiac and a Swiss company aims its marketing effort specifically at the impotent.

Lyall believes that pollen stimulates the regeneration of tissue and accelerates metabolism, thereby slowing down the process of aging. Orthodox nutritionists, however, point out that, as in honey, the vitamins and other beneficial substances in pollen are present in such small amounts as to be useless. There is nothing in pollen, they say, that is not to be found in a balanced diet.

And what of those 120 year old patriarchs in Colombia, Georgia and Pakistan? Beehive scrap is no doubt a valuable food, but these societies share other characteristics. They are mountain peoples, whose life style combines hard physical work with a low level of stress. They all eat large quantities of yogurt. And, perhaps, most importantly of all, their cultural values do not include the attitude that one should slow down or give up in old age. These factors, in combination with genetic traits and the consumption of beehive scrap, may all play a part in enhancing the longevity of these remarkable people. Although a beguiling idea, the claims that beehive scrap alone plays a significant role remain to be demonstrated.

Some recent old wives' tales have evolved in connection with royal jelly or bee milk. We saw in Chapter 3 that this secretion of the mandibular and hypopharyngeal glands of worker honeybees is fed to the larvae for the first three or four days of life. Larvae which are destined to be queens continue to be fed exclusively on royal jelly for the rest of their development, while those destined to become workers are fed a mixture of pollen and honey after the third or fourth day. (Plate 13-2)

The fact that honeybee larvae which are fed entirely on royal jelly become fertile queens instead of sterile workers has captured the imaginations of the copywriters of advertisements for face creams said to contain the magical substance. In a modern expression of the Doctrine of Signatures, the advertisers grow lyrical on the rejuvenating effects of royal jelly on bees. Queen bees, they remind us, live 1600 times as long as the workers. One expensive preparation is designed to revitalize "tired" skin and prevent the formation of wrinkles. The active ingredient is said to be royal jelly with its well known feminizing effects on bee larvae. This is, of course, a complete fallacy, for the implication is that femininity in bees, that is, the ability to lay eggs, has biochemical equivalence to femininity in women, that well known but poorly understood mixture of intangibles.

Several commercially available elixirs contain royal jelly and are claimed to have rejuvenating effects. However, no amount of endorsement by famous romantic novelists will make it anything other than it is, a rich food for bee larvae which has no important substances that are absent from a normal, balanced, healthy human diet.

Royal jelly may, however, come to have legitimate use in medicine. There are encouraging results in research on atherosclerosis, the furring up of arteries with fatty deposits. In animals with experimentally induced atherosclerosis, those treated with royal jelly as a dietary supplement developed the disease more slowly than did untreated ones.

There has always been a belief that arthritis can be relieved by bee venom; beekeepers, with their unavoidable experience of stings, are said to be singularly free from arthritic disease. Modern medicine has investigated these claims and has had to swallow its pride, for extract of whole bee venom has been used effectively in the treatment of this painful and often crippling disease. (see Plate 13-1) A team at Guy's Hospital, London, showed that one component of honeybee venom, peptide 401, is 100 times more effective in reducing inflammation of the joints than hydrocortisone, one of the drugs commonly used in therapy. Peptide 401 has an additional advantage in that it has none of the undesirable side effects which bedevil treatment with steroids such as hydrocortisone. Although bee venom therapy is available in some medical centers in Britain and North America, it is still unfashionable, perhaps because the drug companies can make larger profits by peddling more expensive compounds.

Another old wives' tale has recently been vindicated. Many old beekeepers claim that propolis, the sticky gum based on resins collected by worker honeybees from bud scales, is a sure preventative for a variety of ills. I knew one Oxfordshire beekeeper who always chews a few pellets of propolis when he feels a cold coming on. Recent studies of this substance proved that it is rich in vitamin C, which the body requires to fight infections as well as in the manufacture of collagen. More detailed studies showed that extract of propolis increased the rate of phagocytosis, the process by which the white blood cells ingest invading disease organisms.

As medical scientists research more fully into bee products, there is no doubt that they will find some potentially useful drugs. Nevertheless, we should make a distinction between legitimate claims, backed by double-blind trials and some of the wilder excesses already mentioned. The history of folk medicine is rich in examples of substances or foods, which, because of their exotic or esoteric origins, were believed to have magical powers. Tea, coffee, tomatoes and even the potato were said to have potent medicinal properties when they first became available. The rapidity with which royal jelly was taken up by naturopaths, herbalists and, latterly, the cosmetics industry, is a good example of what I like to call the rhino horn syndrome; for royal jelly, like rhino horn, another alleged aphrodisiac, is obscure in origin and difficult to collect, two factors which seem common to many allegedly powerful natural remedies.

Plate 14-1

Bee Projects: Becoming a Backyard Bee Scientist

14

Plate 14–2

220

Bees: A Natural History

In the British Isles domestic gardens collectively occupy a larger area than all designated nature reserves combined. They are therefore a resource that can be harnessed to further the cause of bee conservation. This is important in a country where most natural flower-rich habitats have fallen prey to intensive agriculture.

By contrast, Canada and the United States still have considerable areas of wild lands, where native floras and natural habitats flourish, often in vast National Parks. Nevertheless, there is no room for complacency. As we saw in Chapter 10, the Central Valley of California is a cause for concern and other areas of the USA suffer the negative effects of intensive, corporate agriculture.

Gardens, with their contrived floral diversity and structural complexity are thus ideal sites for the individual to make a significant contribution to bee conservation.

Plate 14-1. Andrew Coté, 38 years old, is the founder of the New York City Beekeepers' Association, created in December 2008 and which is rapidly growing, bringing together experienced and beginner beekeepers and also all bee lovers. Urban beekeeping is a growing hobby in large cities such as New York, London and Paris. Credit: Éric Tourneret. (see page 218)

Plate 14-2. A sweat bee *Halictus scabiosae* visits a *Eryngium campestre* blossom, Cévennes Mountains, France. Many species of this genus are eusocial with colony sizes ranging from very small (2–4) to large (over 200). Like many halictid mining bees, this widespread, primitively eusocial Eurasian species excavates nests along the margins of paths or in fine-grained compacted soil. Credit: Henk Wallays.

Individuals really can make a difference. In 2013, HRH Prince Charles planted 60 flower-rich hay meadows, to mark the 60th anniversary of the Coronation of his mother, Queen Elizabeth II. The meadows will be managed to maintain floral diversity for the benefit of insect pollinators and will augment his efforts in the grounds of Highgrove, his country residence.

One, however, doesn't need the resources of the British Royal Family to be able to make a significant contribution: one of the simplest ways of enhancing the lot of wild bees is to create a bee garden which includes an area of lawn set aside as a hay meadow. This can be achieved with bee-friendly seed mixes now widely available from nurseries and garden centers:

- In late spring or early summer, clear an area of grass and rake over to form a fine tilth.

- Scatter the seeds and water them in. They will soon germinate, flower and start to attract bees and other pollinators, such as hoverflies and butterflies.

- In late summer mow this small but important meadow. This will scatter the seeds of annuals for next year and stimulate the growth of biennials and perennials.

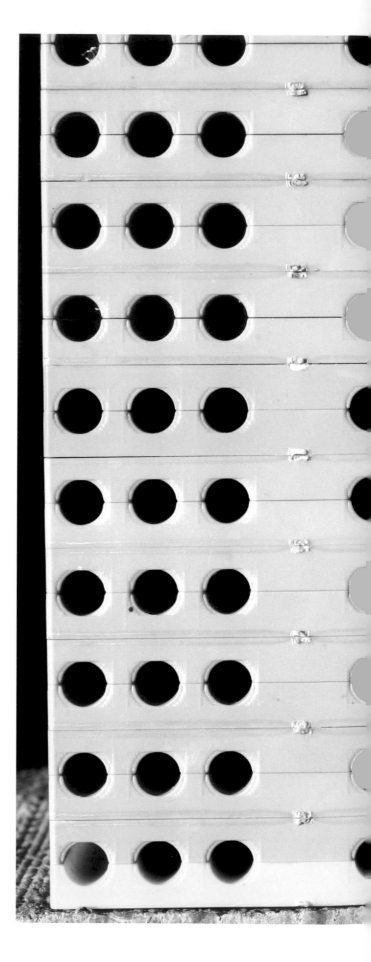

Plate 14-3. Two commercially available nests designs for cavity-nesting bees masons, leafcutters and carders. That on the left, designed by Margaret Dogterom, comprises a stack of interlocking grooved plates. These can easily be separated at the end of the nesting season for the examination of contents as part of research studies. The nest on the left comprises a plastic canister containing cardboard tubes, each with a removable paper liner. Both contain completed nests sealed by females of the Eurasian Red Mason bee, *Osmia rufa.* Credit: Christopher O'Toole.

Bees: A Natural History

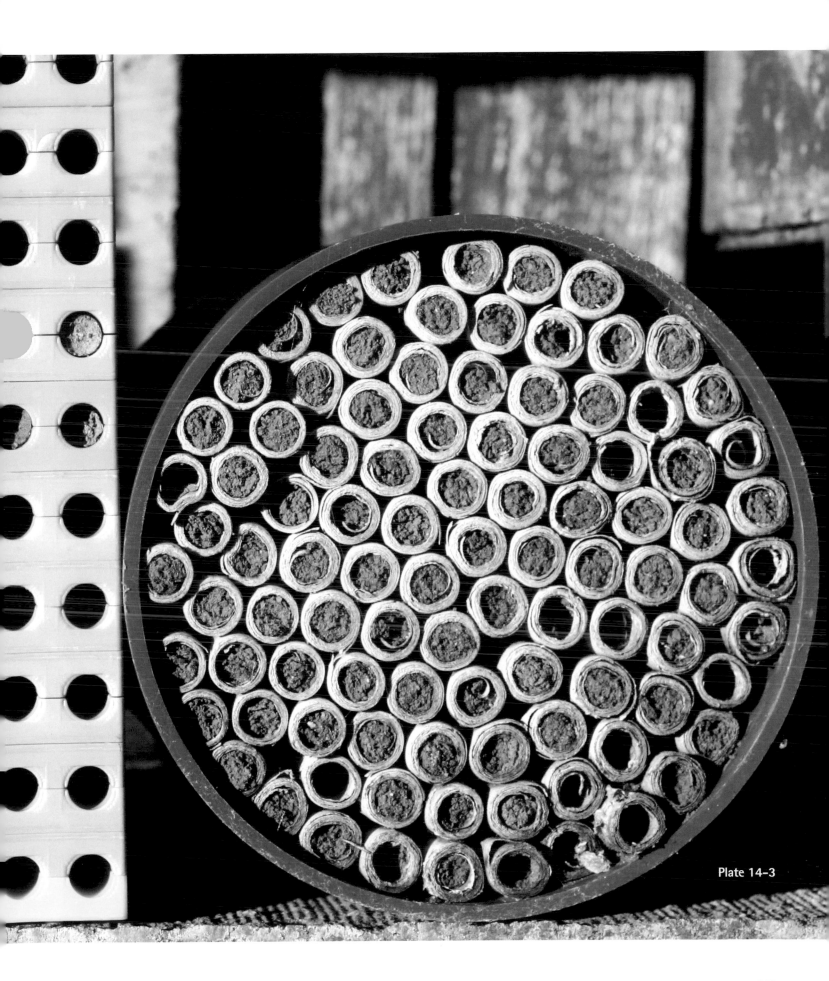

Plate 14-3

Bee Projects: Becoming a Backyard Bee Scientist

In more formal flower beds, it's worth trying to grow a wide range of flowers that bees like. A combination of shallow and deep-tubed flowers will cater for the nectar needs of both short and long-tongued bees.

An easy way to decide what to grow is to have a look at local public gardens and see which flowers seem most attractive to bees. The combination of plants which grows best on a particular plot will depend on soil type and aspect. (Plate 14-1)

Things to avoid

Double or treble-flowered varieties of plants: especially roses and dahlias, chrysanthemums and marigolds. They may look attractive but, according to type, the nectaries and/or anther-bearing stamens have been converted by selective breeding into extra whorls of petals. The result is a plant which has no resources to attract and sustain bees. In some cases, extra whorls of petals make it difficult or impossible for bees to gain access to any remaining anthers or nectaries. Such varieties therefore cannot reproduce in the normal way and are propagated by planting tubers or taking cuttings.

Chipped bark mulches: these reduce the amount of bare ground available for mining bees. If weeds are a major problem, then compromise - retain at least some areas of bare soil and nest sites.

Other compromises are also desirable: try and tolerate some wild flowers in marginal areas. Dandelions (*Taraxacum* spp.*)*, usually regarded as weeds, are excellent sources of nectar and pollen for early spring bees on both sides of the Atlantic. They are a useful resource at a time of the year when the weather can be unpredictable and the number of consecutive days available for foraging can be limited. As an added bonus, their fresh leaves add piquancy to salads.

Bees are very good at finding rich food resources and a well-stocked garden will soon be busy with foraging bees.

Providing nest sites is the next step in becoming a backyard bee scientist. Patches of bare earth will attract nest seeking female bees, especially mining bees such as species of *Andrena*, *Halictus* and *Lasioglossum*, the latter two genera favoring fine-grained, compacted earth, especially along the margins of paths. For those species which prefer to nest on an incline, compacted earth banks facing south or south-west will be useful.

Mining bees in the genera *Anthophora* and *Habropoda* (North America and Eurasia) and *Amegilla* (Eurasia, Australia, Africa) often prefer to nest in vertical or near vertical clay cliffs and will also nest in the mortar of old walls or in adobe bricks. This can be reproduced in the backyard setting:

- Make a mix of coarse sand and cement, roughly in the ratio of 2/3 sand to 1/3 cement.

- Add water to make a dense paste, mix thoroughly and compact into suitable containers such as plastic storage boxes sold in supermarkets with the dimensions 45cm x 36cm x 24.5cm (17.7 x 14 x 9.6 inches).

- Ensure that the surface of the "adobe" mix is about 3.5cm (1.4 inches) lower than the handgrip holes.

- Before the "adobe" mix is completely dry, use an index finger to make starter holes in the surface, ensuring that each hole is separated from its nearest neighbor by at least 5cm (2 inches). The starter holes will encourage nest-seeking females to investigate and make trial excavations.

- When the "adobe" mix is dry, turn the container on its long side on some support so that it is at least 30.5cm (12 inches) above ground. Cinder blocks (breeze blocks) are ideal.

- Place the nest block in a sunny situation, facing south or south-east.

Female mining bees in the genera *Anthophora* and *Amegilla* have mandibles and forelegs which are sufficiently robust to excavate this material. Female Long-horned bees (*Eucera* spp.) (North America and Eurasia) may also use these adobe-type nest blocks.

Plate 14-4

Plate 14-4. Females of the widespread North American Blue Orchard bee, *Osmia lignaria*, at their nest entrances, warming up in the early morning sun, Kern County, California. This species takes readily to these artificial nests. Three simple eyes (ocelli) are visible between the compound eyes. Credit: Christopher O'Toole. (See Appendix 1 for suppliers of nests)

Bombus hypnorum

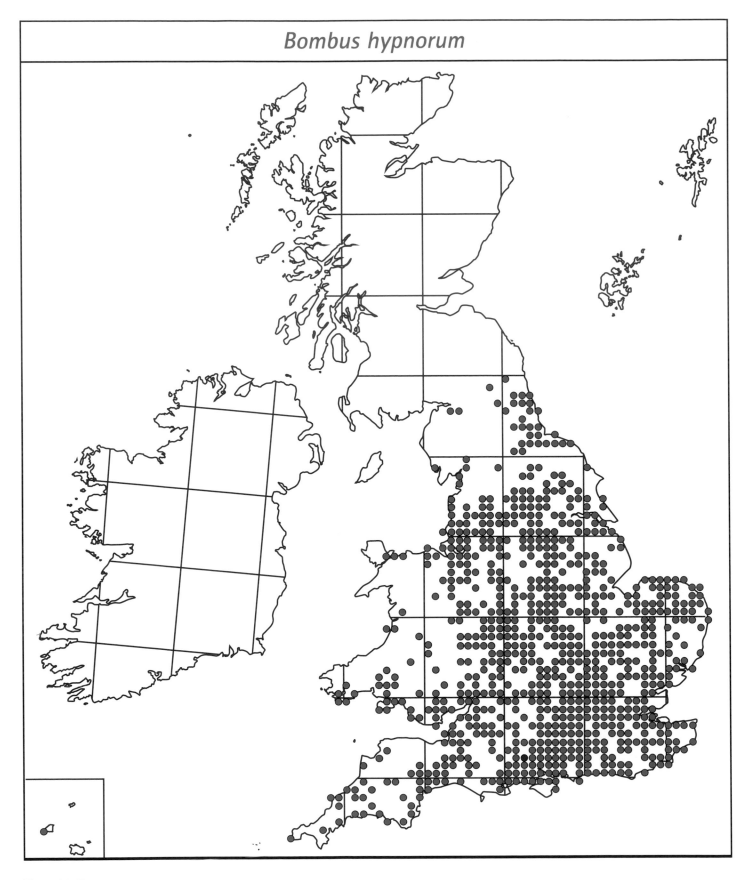

Plate 14-5

Bees: A Natural History

It is easier to provide nest sites for cavity nesting bees such as the leafcutter, mason and carder bees (*Megachile, Osmia, Anthidium* spp.; see Chapter 3) and there are a number of options. (Plate 14-4)

The simplest is to drill holes in the cut ends of timber. Pine and other fine-grained soft woods are best. Most wood yards will give away off-cuts to budding bee scientists. Fine-grained hard woods such as oak are also suitable, though they are harder to drill into and require patience: at high speeds, drill bits get hot and the smell of scorched wood may put off some nest-seeking bees, so I recommend low speed drill settings. Holes should be 15–18cm (6–7 inches) deep.

Another option is to bundle together lengths of hollow bamboo (15–18cm/6-7 inches) and suspend them on wooden sheds with the opening of the bundle flush with the edge of a wall.

It is useful to provide a range of nest diameters to reflect the preferences of as wide a range of cavity-nesters as possible: the bees' choice is related to their body size. For most leafcutters, masons and carders, a range from 5–12mm (0.25–0.5") will suffice.

Several commercially available nest kits are available. (Plate 14-3) These have been designed primarily for leafcutters and mason bees and have a smaller range of nest diameters usually 7.5–8mm.

With a flower-rich garden and an array of nests, the last step in becoming a backyard bee scientist is to join a special interest group which fosters the conservation and

study of bees. Such groups organize projects in which people can participate. These include recording which bees are found in gardens and collaborating in surveys of the distribution of bees (see Appendix 2).

One of the best examples is the North American Great Sunflower Project, which has been running for five years. Administered by San Francisco University, it has about 100,000 volunteers across the country. They count the number of bees present in their back yards in a regular 15-minute period of observation over several months. Sunflowers (*Helianthus* spp.) do not have to be the only plants on which counts are based. Suggested alternatives are Purple Coneflower (*Echinacea purpurea*), Tickseed (*Coreopsis* spp.), Cosmos (*Cosmos* spp.), Bee balm (*Monarda* spp.) and Rosemary (*Rosmarinus officinalis*). The information submitted by these backyard bee scientists has supported the work of university bee scientists in their analysis of where bee populations are strongest or weakest.

In Britain, the Bees Wasps and Ant Recording Society has played a similar role for many years. Because Britain is much smaller than the United States and its bee fauna is minute in comparison, 271 species compared to 5,000, it has been possible to map the distribution of bees with some accuracy. In collaboration with the Biological Records Centre, the society publishes maps with a resolution down to a 10km (6-mile) square (Plate 14-5) and the records are not limited to domestic gardens.

The bees attracted to gardens by the above suggestions are safe with children and pets. They are docile because, unlike the honeybee, they do not have large numbers of larvae and honey stores to protect. It is fascinating to watch a variety of different bees going about their business at flowers and nests and there is great pleasure in knowing how easy it is to make a difference in the conservation of these useful and often beautiful insects. (see Plate 14-4)

Plate 14-5. The current (Spring 2013) known distribution of the Eurasian Tree bumblebee, *Bombus hypnorum*. The species has spread rapidly since its first discovery in southern Britain in 2001. Each dot on the map represents a 10km (6-mile) square in which the bee has been recorded, largely by amateur enthusiasts, members of the British Bees Wasps and Ant Recording Society (BWARS). This map demonstrates not only the rapid northward spread of this bee, but also what can be achieved in bee research by the collaboration of enthusiastic backyard bee scientists. Credit: Biological Records Center/ BWARS.

Worker stingless bees, *Trigona* spp., gathering nectar at a passion flower, *Passiflora* sp. Passion flowers are structurally adapted for pollination by large carpenter bees, *Xylocopa* spp. Being too small to pollinate this kind of flower, the stingless bees are simply robbing the flower of nectar. Peru. Credit: Edward Ross.

Appendix 1: Suppliers of products for bee projects

UNITED STATES and CANADA

Bee Diverse
Phone: (604) 936-3919
Fax: (604) 936-3927
Out of town toll free:1-800-794-2144
www.beediverse.com.
Film of Blue Orchard Bees, Osmia lignaria, at nests called
"Quicklock Nesting Trays for Mason Bees."
http://www.youtube.com/watch?v=d-FoRqvyk3c

Knox Cellars
PO Box 28396,
Bellingham, WA 98228
orders@knoxcellars.com
https://www.knoxcellars.com/Merchant5/merchant.
mvc?Screen=SFNT&Store_Code=KCNP

Orcon
P. O. Box 781147W
Los Angeles, CA 90016
Phone: (323) 937-7444
Fax: (323) 937-0123
http://organiccontrol.com/category/bees/bee_nest/

UNITED KINGDOM and EUROPE

CJ Wildbird Foods
CJ Wildlife,
The Rea,
Upton Magna,
Shrewsbury SY4 4UR

UNITED KINGDOM
Toll-free in the UK: 0800 731 2820
Fax: (0)1743 709504
http://www.birdfood.co.uk/products.php?area_
id=2&nav_id=47

Wildlife World
Manor Farm Barn,
Chavenage,
Nr. Tetbury,
Gloucestershire GL8 8XW
UNITED KINGDOM
Email: info@wildlifeworld.co.uk
http://www.wildlifeworld.co.uk/bee_habitats_range.html

Appendix 2: Bee-related web sites

The following are web sites of organizations with an active interest in the conservation of bees. They are a rich source of well-illustrated information and ideas for projects which individuals can set up to enhance our knowledge of bees, their seasonal activity, floral relations and distribution.

http://www.xerces.org/pollinator-resource-center/
[North America – excellent source of regionally based information about plant lists, habitat conservation guides, projects, literature]

http://www.greatsunflower.org/
[The world's largest citizen science project focussing on pollinator conservation, with many excellent and informative links; includes slide show of commonest North American bees.]

http://www.helpabee.org and http://nature.berkeley.edu/urbanbeegardens/
[Excellent web sites for ideas on plantings for the creation of bee gardens]

http://ucce.ucdavis.edu/files/repositoryfiles/ca6303p113-72518.pdf
[An excellent overview of urban bees in California, with ideas which can be applied in other states]

http://www.pollinatorparadise.com/
[North America - comprehensive, with many useful links and ideas]

http://www.bwars.com/
[Bees Ants and Wasps Recording Society, United Kingdom]

http://bumblebeeconservation.org/
[Bumblebee Conservation Trust, United Kingdom – current bumblebee news, project ideas]

http://www.ibra.org.uk/
[International Bee Research Association - collects, collates and disseminates information on all species of bees. Also a publishing house for bee books and scientific journals devoted to bee research.]

http://www.atlashymenoptera.net/start.htm
[Belgium, France]

http://wildbienen.info/
[The website of Dr Paul Westrich, a leading European authority on bees; excellent images of bees]

http://www.nev.nl/hymenoptera/index.html
[The Netherlands]

http://www.wildbienen-kataster.de/
[Germany]

http://pinterest.com/siddal/hive-heart/
[Eclectic assemblage of bee ephemera]

http://andrewgough.co.uk
[Bees and people through the ages]

http://www.orchidstudium.com
[Information and many photographs of tropical orchids discussed in Chapter 8 Bees and Orchids]

Further reading

The following references have good general accounts of the diversity of bees and their natural history and are particularly relevant to Chapters 1-5 and 9.

Michener, C. D., 2007. *The Bees of the World* (2nd ed.). The Johns Hopkins University Press, Baltimore. 953pp.

O'Toole, C. and Raw, A., 1991. *Bees of the World*. Blandford (Cassell), London. 192pp.

Roubik, D. W., 1989. *Ecology and Natural History of Tropical Bees*. Cambridge University Press, Cambridge. 514pp.

Selected references by chapter

Chapter 1: The Wasp Inheritance
Grimaldi, D. and Engel, M. S., 2005. *Evolution of the Insects*. Cambridge University Press, New York. 755pp.

Chapter 2: The Business of Being a Bee
Frisch, K. von. 1974. *Animal Architecture*. [With the collaboration of Otto von Frisch] Harcourt Brace Jovanovich, San Diego, California. 306pp.

Michener, C. D., 2007. *The Bees of the World* (2nd ed.). The Johns Hopkins University Press, Baltimore. 953pp.

O'Toole, C. and Raw, A., 1991. *Bees of the World*. Blandford (Cassell), London. 192pp.

Chapter 3: Solitary Bees
O'Toole, C., 2002. *The Red Mason Bee, Osmia rufa: all you need to know....* Osmia Publications, Rothley. 40pp.

O'Toole. C. 2010. *The Blue Orchard Bee, Osmia lignaria*. Osmia Publications, Sileby. 34pp.

Chapter 4: Social bees
Benton, T.,, *Bumblebees*. Collins New Naturalist Series, 98. Collins, London. 580pp.

Breed, M. D., Michener, C. D. and Evans, H. E., 1982. *The Biology of Social Insects*. Westview Press, Boulder, Co. 419pp.

Brian, M. V., 1983. *Social Insects: Ecology and Behavioural Biology*. Chapman and Hall, London. 377pp.

Goulson, D., 2003. *Bumblebees, Their Behaviour and Ecology*. Oxford University Press, Oxford. 235pp.

Frisch, K. von. 1967. *The Dance Language and Orientation of Bees*. Harvard University Press, Cambridge, Mass. 566pp.

Heinrich, B., 1979. *Bumblebee Economics*. Harvard University Press, Cambridge, Mass. 245pp.

Michener, C. D., 1974. *The Social Behavior of the Bees*. Harvard University Press, Cambridge, Mass. 404pp.

Seeley, T. S., 1985. *Honeybee Ecology. A Study of Adaptation to Social Life*. Princeton University Press, Princeton NJ. 201pp.

Winston, M., 1987. *The Biology of the Honeybee*. Harvard University Press, Cambridge, Mass. 281pp.

Chapter 5: The Male of the Species
Blum, M. S. and Blum, N. A. 1979. *Sexual Selection and Reproductive Competition in Insects*. Academic Press, New York. 462pp.

Choe, Jae C., and Bernard J. Crespi, eds., 1997. *The Evolution of Mating Systems in Insects and Arachnids*. Cambridge. 387pp. University Press, Cambridge,. *Cambridge Books Online*. Web. 23 May 2013.http://dx.doi.org/10.1017/CBO9780511721946

Thornhill, R. and Alcock, J., 2001. *The Evolution of Insect Mating Systems*. Harvard University Press, Cambridge, Mass. 547pp. http://www.bbc.co.uk/nature/life/Amegilla#p0053k73

Chapters 6: The Pollination Market
Buchmann, S. and Nabhan, G., 1997. *The Forgotten Pollinators*. Island Press, Washington, D.C. 344pp.

Chambers, N., Gray, Y. and Buchmann, S., 2004. *Pollinators of the Sonoran Desert*. Arizona - Sonora Desert Museum – International Sonoran Desert Alliance – The Bee Works. 83pp.

Dafni, A., 1992., *Pollination Ecology – A Practical Approach*. IRL Press at Oxford University Press, Oxford. 250pp.

Free, J. B., 1970. *Insect Pollination of Crops*. Academic Press, London. 544pp.

Heinrich, B., 2004. *Bumblebee Economics*. Harvard University Press, Cambridge. MA. 280pp.

James, R. R. and Pitts-Singer, T. L., (eds) 2008. *Bee Pollination in Agricultural Ecosystems*. Oxford University Press, New York. 232pp.

Meeuse, B. and Morris, S., 1984. *The Sex Life of Flowers*. Faber and Faber, London. 152pp.

Proctor, M., Yeo, P. and Lack, A., 1996. *The Natural History of Pollination*. Harper Collins New Naturalist Series, London. 479pp.

Chapter 7: Squash Bees and Other Pollen Specialists
Barth, F. G., 1985 (Translated by M. A. Biederman-Thorson). *Insects and Flowers – The Biology of a Partnership*. George Allen & Unwin (UK)/Princetron University Press, USA. 297pp.

Chambers, N., Gray, Y. and Buchmann, S., 2004. *Pollinators of the Sonoran Desert*. Arizona - Sonora Desert Museum – International Sonoran Desert Alliance – The Bee Works. 83pp.

Waser, N. M. and Ollerton, J., 2006. *Plant-Pollinator Interactions: From Specialization to Generalization*. The University of Chicago Press, Chicago. 445pp.

Chapter 8: Bees and Orchids
Meeuse, B. and Morris, S., 1984. *The Sex Life of Flowers*. Faber and Faber, London. 152pp.

Proctor, M., Yeo, P. and Lack, A., 1996. *The Natural History of Pollination*. Harper Collins New Naturalist Series, London. 479pp.

Roubik, D. W. and Hanson, P. E., 2004. *Orchid Bees of Tropical America: Biology and Field Guide*. Instituto Nacional de Biodiversidad – Smithsonian Institution. Santo Domingo de Heredia, Costa Rica. 370pp.

Chapter 9: Enemies and Associates
See page 232 under "Further reading."

Chapter 10: The Conservation and Management of Bees
Bosch, J. and Kemp, W., 2001. *How to Manage the Blue Orchard Bee as an Orchard Pollinator*. Sustainable Agriculture Network, Handbook 5, National Agriculture Library, Beltsville, MD. 88pp.

Delaplane, K. S. and Mayer, D. F., 2000. *Crop Pollination by Bees*. CABI Publishing, Wallingford. 344pp.

Nabhan, G.P. and Buchmann, S., 1997. Services provided by Pollinators. in Daily, G. (ed) 1997. *Nature's Services: Societal Dependence on Natural Ecosystems*. Island Press, Washington, D.C. 392pp.

Packer, L., 2010. *Keeping the Bees: Why all bees are at risk and what we can do to save them*. Harper-Collins, Toronto. 273pp.

Chapter 11: Bees and People — Historical
Crane, E., 1999. *The World History of Beekeeping and Honey Hunting*. Duckworth, London. 682pp.

Ransome, H. M., 1937. *The sacred bee in ancient times and folklore.* George Allen and Unwin, London. (Facsimile reprint 1986, Burrowbridge: Bee Book New and Old).

Chapter 12: Bees in Folklore

Cotton, W. C., 1842. *My Bee Book.* Rivington, London. (Kingsmead Reprints, 1970).

Crane, E., 1999. *The World History of Beekeeping and Honey Hunting.* Duckworth, London. 682pp.

Ransome, H. M., 1937. *The sacred bee in ancient times and folklore.* George Allen and Unwin, London. (Facsimile reprint 1986, Burrowbridge: Bee Book New and Old).

Chapter 13: Bees in Folk and Modern Medicine

Ransome, H. M., 1937. *The sacred bee in ancient times and folklore.* George Allen and Unwin, London. (Facsimile reprint 1986, Burrowbridge: Bee Book New and Old).

Crane, E., 1999. *The World History of Beekeeping and Honey Hunting.* Duckworth, London. 682pp.

Chapter 14: Bee Projects – Becoming a Backyard Bee Scientist

Dogterom, M., 2002. *Pollination with Mason Bees: A Gardener's Guide to Managing Mason Bees for Fruit Production.* Beediverse Books, Coquitlam, BC Canada. 80pp.

Grissell, E., 2010. *Bees, Wasps, and Ants: The Indispensable Role of Hymenoptera in Gardens.* Timber Press, Portland, OR. 336pp.

Mader, E., Spivak, Marla, Evans, E. 2010. *Managing Alternative Pollinators: A Handbook for Beekeepers, Growers, and Conservationists.* The Xerces Society/ Sustainable Agriculture, Research and Education, University of Maryland. 162pp.

Mader, E., Shepherd, M., Vaughn, M., Black, S., in collaboration with LeBuhn, G. 2011. *Attracting Native Pollinators: Protecting North America's Bees and Butterflies.* The Xerces Society/Storey Publishing, North Adams MA. 380pp.

O'Toole, C., 2002. *The Red Mason Bee, Osmia rufa: all you need to know....* Osmia Publications, Rothley. 40pp.

O'Toole. C. 2010. *The Blue Orchard Bee, Osmia lignaria.* Osmia Publications, Sileby. 34pp.

O'Toole, C. 2012. *Plants for Solitary Bees* in Kirk, W. D. and Howes, F. N., (eds) *Plants for Bees.* International Bee Research Association, Cardiff. 311pp.

Acknowledgments

I am grateful to my wife Rose for her eagle-eyed reading of the manuscript of this book and her many helpful suggestions. Her support for this project was heroic given the serious illness she suffered during its writing.

Our very dear friends Elizabeth Jacobs, Stella and Julie Chinn, Nick Lintott and Pauline and Richard Corfield provided huge, generous and always timely levels of support for Rose and me.

Other friends gave practical support in very many ways and I thank Patti, Richard and Lynne Bailey, Martin and Sophie Barnes, Sue Barry, Paul Fenwick and Lyn Hodges, Alan Jones, Roger Knott, Jami Mahboubi, Jane Riddles, David and Annie Schonveld, Amanda Soraghan and Anne and Rob Swann. In helping us through the long and difficult period of Rose's treatment, all of these friends helped create space and time for me to write.

I am very grateful to my brother Peter for his valuable advice on matters photographic and for his companionship in the field.

I also thank my friends and colleagues in Israel, Amots Dafni, Avi Shmida, Hagar Leschner and Achik Dorchin, who, over the years, have made it possible for me to study and collect bees in a wide range of habitats. I am grateful to Dr Jim Cane of the USDA Bee Systematics and Biology Laboratory, Dr. Mark O'Neill and Ian Nicholson for reading over parts of the manuscript.

Andy Marmoys kept my computer going and I am grateful to him for much help.

Finally, I thank Peter Névraumont of the Névraumont Publishing Company, New York, not only for his editorial wisdom, but also for his patience and understanding. I am also grateful to Lionel Koffler and his staff at Firefly Books for their continuing support for this project and to Nicholas LiVolsi for his elegant book design.

Christopher O'Toole,
Loughborough, September 2013

Index

abdomen (bee), 9, 10, 14, 17, 19, 21, 26, 28, 31, 36, 44, 51, 52, 57, 61, 70, 72, 74, 80, 81, 82, 86, 89, 100

aerodynamics, 9

Agapostemon, 8, 42,

Aglae, 38

Alcock, John , 98

Alfalfa Leafcutter bee, 10, 61, 112, 170, 171, 173

alfalfa, 10, 54, 112, 166, 169, 170, 171

alkali bee, 52, 54, 73, 170

Allodape, 36

Ambrose, J.T., 199

Amegilla, 36, 48, 118, 224; *albocaudata*, 173, *asserta*, 171, 174; *calens*, 173; *chryososseles*, 173

Andrena, 27, 41, 54, 72, 107, 117, 146, 155, 159, 160, 163, 224; *bucephala*, 72; *carantonica*, 70, 72; *erythronii*, 127; *ferox*, 72; *flavipes*, 38; *florae*, 128; nigroaenea, 147; *vaga*, 147; *vetula*, 57, 98

Andrenidae, 29, 41, 52. 117, 121

antennae (bee), 16, 36, 97, 141

Anthidiellum notatum, 65

Anthidium, 41, 117, 227; *maculosum*, 65; *manicatum*, 65, 66, 101, 117

Anthophora, 36, 54, 57, 99, 117, 128, 224; *bomboides*, 16, 48, 52, 94, 99; *erschowi*, 97; *fulvitarsis*, 57; *hermanni*, 51; *plumipes*, 57, 58, 98, 173; *romandii*, 52, 54, 57; *senescens*, 57

Anthophoridae, 52

Apidae, 26. 29, 33, 36, 81, 117, 118, 121, 126

Apinae, 26

Apis, 26, 38, 82, 94, 103; *andreniformis*, 118; *binghami*, 118; *breviligula*, 118; *cerana*, 118, 187, 188, 189, 193; *dorsata*, 191, 193; *florae*, 118; *koschevnikovi*, 118; *laboriosa*, 191; *mellifera*, 5, 19, 26, 35, 38, 81, 82, 83, 85, 88, 103, 114, 118, 187, 188, 189, 207; *nigrocincta*, 118; *nuluensis*, 118

apple, 109, 120, 123, 174

Arthropoda, 26

artificial nest, 65, 155, 171, 173, 174, 226

Ashmeadiella, 41

Augochloropsis, 42, 70, 107 *diversipennis*, 70; *mettalica*, 107; *sparsillis*, 73

bactericide, 213

basistarsis, 27

"bee-bob", 199

bee sting, 19, 52, 70, 72, 85, 212

Bee Wolf wasp, 15

bee, native, 38, 101, 126, 166, 168, 170, 171, 174, 179, 188

bee, swarm, 82, 86-8, 91, 98, 103, 187, 196, 197-9, 206, 207

bee, wild, 10, 82, 126, 166, 168, 179, 183, 187, 192, 206, 207, 222

beehive, 8, 20, 81, 85, 86, 87, 114, 118, 125, 152, 162, 169. 170, 187, 188, 190, 191-9, 201-2, 206-9, 212, 215, 216, 221

beekeeping, 10, 82, 85, 155, 157, 169, 187, 188, 190-1, 197-9, 201-3, 205-7, 209, 217, 221

beeswax, 76, 79, 81-2, 85, 87-8, 91, 94, 131, 183, 188, 192-3, 199, 202, 206, 213

beetle, 15, 82, 102, 126, 134; borings, 10, 42, 65, 155; hive, 168; oil, 155, 157, 159-60; pollination, 107

behavior, 10, 20, 31, 33, 48, 52, 54, 85, 95, 96, 109, 141, 177, 188, 190,197; 23, 155; altruistic, 91; collecting, 141; foraging, 10, 141; gathering, 109; male, 101, 103, 140; mating, 8, 16, 114; nesting, 10, 33; social, 72, 75, 81, 91; territorial, 98; worker, 75

bellflower, 127

Bhramari Devi (Indian bee goddess), 196, 206

biodiversity, 8, 11, 31, 144, 168, 183

Biological Records Centre, 227

bivoltine, 48

Blue Orchard bee, 10, 65, 97, 155, 160, 171, 173, 174, 176, 179, 180, 226, 228, 230, 231, 232

Bombus (bumblebees), 22, 38, 76, 94, 138, 146, 163; *americanum*, 137; *brevivillus*, 138; *hortorum* , 166, 180; *huntii*, 32; *hypnorum*, 76, 225; *lucorum*, 120, 123; *medius*, 79; *occidentalis*, 76; *pascuorum*, 120; *pullatus*. 98; *ruderatus*, 166; *subterraneus*, 166, 168; *terrestris*, 109, 117; *vestalis*, 146; *vosnesenskyii*, 8, 110

brain (bee), 16, 22, 27, 212

Brazil nut, 11, 142, 144, 149, 190

British Bees Wasps and Ant Recording Society (BWARS), 225, 229

brood cell, 16, 41, 48, 52, 65, 66, 75, 76, 79, 82, 94, 128. 129, 154, 155, 163, 193

bryony, 128